OSPREY
PUBLISHING

Battle of the Bulge 1944 (2)

Bastogne

D1288211

Campaign • 145

OSPREY
PUBLISHING

Battle of the Bulge 1944 (2)

Bastogne

Steven J Zaloga • Illustrated by Peter Dennis & Howard Gerrard

Series editor Lee Johnson • Consultant editor David G Chandler

First published in Great Britain in 2004 by Osprey Publishing,
Midland House, West Way, Botley, Oxford OX2 0PH, UK
443 Park Avenue South, New York, NY 10016, USA
Email: info@ospreypublishing.com

A CIP catalogue record for this book is available from the British Library

ISBN 1 84176 810 3

Editor: Lee Johnson
Design: The Black Spot
Index by Alison Worthington
Maps by The Map Studio
3D bird's-eye views by The Black Spot
Battlescene artwork by Peter Dennis and Howard Gerrard
Originated by The Electronic Page Company, Cwmbran, UK
Printed in China through World Print Ltd.

05 06 07 08 09   10 9 8 7 6 5 4 3 2

For a catalog of all books published by Osprey Military
and Aviation please contact:

NORTH AMERICA
Osprey Direct, 2427 Bond Street,
University Park, IL 60466, USA
E-mail: info@ospreydirectusa.com

ALL OTHER REGIONS
Osprey Direct UK, P.O. Box 140,
Wellingborough, Northants, NN8 2FA, UK
E-mail: info@ospreydirect.co.uk

www.ospreypublishing.com

KEY TO MILITARY SYMBOLS

Artist's Note

Readers may care to note that the original paintings from
which the color plates in this book were prepared are
available for private sale. All reproduction copyright
whatsoever is retained by the Publishers. All enquiries
should be addressed to:

> Howard Gerrard
> 11 Oaks Road
> Tenterden
> Kent
> TN30 6RD
>
> Peter Dennis
> Fieldhead
> The Park
> Mansfield
> Nottinghamshire
> NG18 2AT

The Publishers regret that they can enter into no
correspondence upon this matter.

Author's Note

The author would like to thank the staff of the US Army's
Military History Institute at the Army War College at Carlisle
Barracks, PA, for their kind assistance in the preparation of
this book, especially Mr. Randy Hackenburg and Jay
Graybeal of Special Collections. The photos in this book
are primarily from the US Army's Signal Corps collections
at the US National Archives and Records Administration
(NARA) in College Park, MD. Other photos were located at
the special collections branch of the Military History
Institute, including the 28th Division veterans' collections.
Special thanks also to Rob Plas, Ron Volstad and the other
participants of the TWENOT 2001 Ardennes battlefield tour.

   For brevity, the usual conventions have been used
when referring to American and German units. In the case
of US units, 1/393rd Infantry refers to the 1st Battalion,
393rd Infantry Regiment. In the case of German units,
GR.27 refers to Grenadier Regiment 27.

Glossary

AFAB: Armored Field Artillery Battalion
AIB: Armored Infantry Battalion
CCA, CCB, CCR: Combat Command A, B, Reserve (US armored divisions)
GR: Grenadier Regiment
Jabo: German term for American fighter-bombers
KG: Kampfgruppe (battle group)
PIR: Parachute Infantry Regiment
PzGR: Panzergrenadier Regiment
TF: Task Force
VG Div.: Volksgrenadier Division

CONTENTS

The defeat of the 6th Panzer Army's breakthrough attempts in the St Vith sector shifted the focus of the German Ardennes offensive to the south in the second week of the offensive, with attention increasingly focused on Bastogne. This PzKpfw IV Ausf J from the spearhead of Kampfgruppe Peiper was knocked out by US M10 tank destroyers on the road from Bullingen to Wirtzfeld on 17 December. (NARA)

INTRODUCTION

The German counter-offensive in the Ardennes in December 1944 was the decisive campaign of the war in North-West Europe. Hitler's desperate gamble to reverse the course of the war in the West failed within a fortnight. The earlier volume in this series covered the opening stages of this campaign, focusing on the critical German failures on the northern shoulder along the Elsenborn Ridge and near St Vith.[1] The German attack was heavily weighted towards its right wing, the attack by the 6th Panzer Army towards the Meuse River near Liege. When this assault failed to win a breakthrough, its smaller neighbor, the 5th Panzer Army succeeded in overwhelming the green 106th Infantry Division, opening up a gap in the American lines. During the second week of the Ardennes counter-offensive, Hitler attempted to redeem his failing offensive by exploiting the success of the 5th Panzer Army. Panzer divisions formerly assigned to 6th Panzer Army were shifted towards the rupture in the center. Although the Panzer spearheads managed to penetrate deep behind the American lines, precious time had been lost and American armored reinforcements arrived in the days before Christmas. In a series of hard-fought battles before the Meuse in the final days of the year, the Panzer divisions were decimated and the attack decisively halted. Nevertheless, with the onset of harsh winter weather, it would take a month to finally erase the bulge.

THE STRATEGIC SITUATION

The German Ardennes offensive was conducted by three armies along a 37-mile (60km) front, aimed at splitting the Allied armies by driving all the way to Antwerp. Most senior Wehrmacht commanders doubted that such an ambitious objective could be achieved. A number of commanders proposed an operation with the more limited and practical objective of reaching the Meuse, but this was not formally proposed to Hitler because the chief of the Wehrmacht operations staff recognized that Hitler would reject it out of hand. Borrowing from bridge terms, the German officers called the two options "Little Slam" and "Grand Slam". The "Little Slam" objectives help to explain why the German commanders continued to push their forces forward after Christmas, long after it was clear that Hitler's "Grand Slam" objectives could never be reached.

The attack force was not spread evenly along the front, but weighted very heavily towards the right flank and the 6th Panzer Army. The reasons for this were both the geography of the Ardennes and the timing of the operation. The most direct route across the Meuse River was on the

---

1 Campaign 115 *Battle of the Bulge 1944 (1) St Vith and the Northern Shoulder* (2003)

northern side of the attack, using the road network stretching from the German border to Liege. In the center of the attack zone, there were also routes leading to Liege, but they were more circuitous and stretched for a greater distance. In the southern sector emanating out of Luxembourg, the terrain was too mountainous for rapid mobile operations. Time was a critical element, since the plan assumed that the Allies would begin shifting forces into the Ardennes once the attack began. So the shortest route was inevitably the most attractive route. To succeed, the plan required that the Meuse be reached and crossed within four days. Any longer, and the Allies could bring up enough forces to halt the attack.

The heaviest Panzer forces were allocated to the 6th Panzer Army, including two Waffen-SS Panzer corps and about 60 percent of the armored strength of the entire offensive. The 5th Panzer Army in the center had most of the remainder of the armored force in the form of two weaker Panzer corps. The mission of this force was to protect the left flank of 6th Panzer Army, as well as to seize control of the longer, but still valuable, routes to the Meuse in this sector. The final element of the attack, the 7th Army, had practically no armor at all and was an infantry force better suited to the mountainous terrain in Luxembourg. Given its lack of mobility, there were few expectations that it would play a major role in the breakthrough. Instead of pushing to the northwest like the other two armies, once it overcame the initial border defenses it was to wheel to its left, creating a defensive line against American reinforcements coming from the south.

As has been detailed in the earlier volume in this series, the initial attacks in the northern sector failed. The stereotyped tactics used to punch through the forested border area caused needless delays, and permitted the US Army to conduct a slow, deliberate retreat while bringing in significant infantry reinforcements. The attacks of 1st SS-Panzer Corps failed to make a breakthrough of the US infantry defenses and suffered heavy casualties in the process. The right wing of the 5th Panzer Army used more appropriate infiltration tactics to penetrate the initial American defensive line and managed to trap two of the regiments of the 106th Infantry Division, leading to the largest mass surrender of US troops in Europe in World War II. Having created a massive gap in the American lines, the 5th Panzer Army inserted two of its Panzer divisions to exploit the success. The main problem in this sector was that the breach had not been complete. US forces still held the vital road and rail junction at St Vith, which impeded the full exploitation of the gap since it made it difficult to reinforce the spearhead units. The American troops in the salient at St Vith finally withdrew on 23 December. Having covered these operations in the previous volume in this series, the focus here will be on the operations in the southern and central sectors, primarily the operations of the 5th Panzer Army in the center and the 7th Army in Luxembourg.

CHRONOLOGY

11 October First draft of Ardennes plan, codenamed *Wacht am Rhein*, submitted to Hitler.

04.00, 16 December Infantry in 5th Panzer Army sector begin infiltration over Our River.

05.30, 16 December Operation *Herbstnebel* (Autumn Mist) begins with opening barrages against forward US positions in Ardennes.

06.00, 16 December German preparatory artillery ends, infantry begins advancing.

Afternoon-evening, 16 December Bradley orders 10th Armored Division to Bastogne; Eisenhower agrees to shift XVIII Airborne Corps to Ardennes.

17 December 110th Infantry Regiment HQ overwhelmed in Clerf, gap in American lines is open after nightfall.

Midnight, 17 December Middleton deploys CCR, 9th Armored Division, to block approaches to Bastogne.

Nightfall, 18 December First elements of 101st Airborne arrive in Bastogne.

08.00, 19 December First probes by German reconnaissance units into US defenses on outskirts of Bastogne.

Nightfall, 19 December US defenses in Wiltz overwhelmed by end of day; another road to Bastogne is open.

19 December Eisenhower meets with senior US commanders to plan further responses to German attack.

20 December Eisenhower shifts control of US First and Ninth Army units, except for Middleton's VIII Corps, from Bradley's 12th Army Group to Montgomery's 21st Army Group.

Noon, 20 December Model redeploys the II SS-Panzer Corps from the failed 6th Panzer Army attack to the center.

Morning, 21 December III Corps of Patton's Third Army begins attack to relieve Bastogne.

Afternoon, 21 December 116th Panzer Division reaches Hotton but cannot secure town. Battles for the road junctions on the Tailles plateau begin.

11.30, 22 December German emissaries demand Bastogne's surrender; General McAuliffe replies "Nuts".

Evening, 22 December Bastogne is surrounded when Panzer Lehr Division begins moving towards the Ourthe River.

Night 22/23 December High-pressure front moves into Ardennes bringing clear skies and freezing temperatures.

06.00, 23 December US forces begin withdrawal from St Vith salient.

Late morning, 23 December II SS Panzer Corps begins moving towards Tailles plateau with 2nd SS Panzer Division in the lead.

Evening, 23 December 2nd Panzer Division reports it has reached within 6miles (9km) of Meuse River near Dinant.

Late evening, 23 December 2nd SS Panzer Division *Das Reich* overruns US defenses and seizes Manhay road junction.

25 December Clear weather permits intense Allied air activity.

Morning, 25 December US 2nd Armored Division begins surrounding and destroying advance guard of the 2nd Panzer Division on the approaches to Dinant.

Late afternoon, 26 December Task force from 4th Armored Division punches through German defenses, beginning the relief of Bastogne.

Dawn, 27 December 2nd SS Panzer Division pushed out of Grandmenil and Manhay; 6th Panzer Army ordered over to the defensive.

30 December Germans and Americans plan attacks in Bastogne area; German attacks fail to make headway.

3 January Manteuffel attempts a final attack on Bastogne that fails; last major German attack of the Ardennes campaign. US First Army begins attack towards Houfallize to meet up with Patton's Third Army.

16 January US First Army and US Third Army link up at Houfallize.

28 January The last of the territory lost to the German attack is retaken by US troops.

OPPOSING PLANS

THE GERMAN PLAN

The 5th Panzer Army attack was three corps wide, with the 66th Infantry Corps on the right (northern) wing, the 58th Panzer Corps in the center and the 47th Panzer Corps on the left (southern) wing. The task of the 66th Infantry Corps was to capture the key road junction and town of St Vith, and although the corps succeeded in overwhelming the US 106th Infantry Division, it was unable to seize the town, frustrating its intended mission of closing on the Meuse. The task of the 58th Panzer Corps, consisting of the 116th Panzer Division and the 560th Volksgrenadier Division, was to penetrate the border area and move on the Meuse via Houfallize. The 47th Panzer Corps, consisting of the 2nd Panzer Division and the 26th Volksgrenadier Division, had Bastogne as its target. After taking this vital road center, the corps was to proceed to the Meuse and cross in the area south of the heavily fortified city of Namur. Supporting these three corps was a Panzer reserve consisting of the Panzer Lehr Division and the Führer Begleit Brigade, which would be committed once one of the corps secured a major breakthrough. In the event, the problems in overcoming American resistance at St Vith forced the 5th Panzer Army commander, General Hasso von Manteuffel, to commit the Führer Begleit Brigade prematurely.

Given the limited forces at his disposal, Manteuffel realized that he would have to cut corners to accomplish the mission. If the objective was indeed to lunge past the Meuse, then the objectives stated in the plan could not be taken literally. The attack force was spread too thin to actually seize and hold several of the larger towns and cities such as Bastogne, Houfallize, La Roche and St Vith. Accordingly, Manteuffel made it clear to his subordinates that if stiff resistance was encountered, the Panzer forces were to bypass the towns and leave them for the infantry formations following behind to deal with. While this tactic made sense given the strategic objective of the offensive, in the event it would come back to haunt Manteuffel after the main objective of the Meuse River proved to be out of reach, since it left a major obstruction, Bastogne, as a center of resistance in his rear.

Manteuffel's deployment plan was different from that of the neighboring 6th Panzer Army under SS-Obergruppenführer Sepp Dietrich, which was echeloned in depth along very narrow attack corridors. Manteuffel believed that such an approach was foolhardy in view of the lack of adequate roads in the Ardennes, and much as he predicted, the SS-Panzer divisions quickly became bogged down in traffic jams once the attack began. His approach was to deploy his units more broadly on the basis that "if we knocked on ten doors, we would find several open". In the event, his tactics proved far more successful than Dietrich's.

GERMAN OBJECTIVES SOUTHERN SECTOR

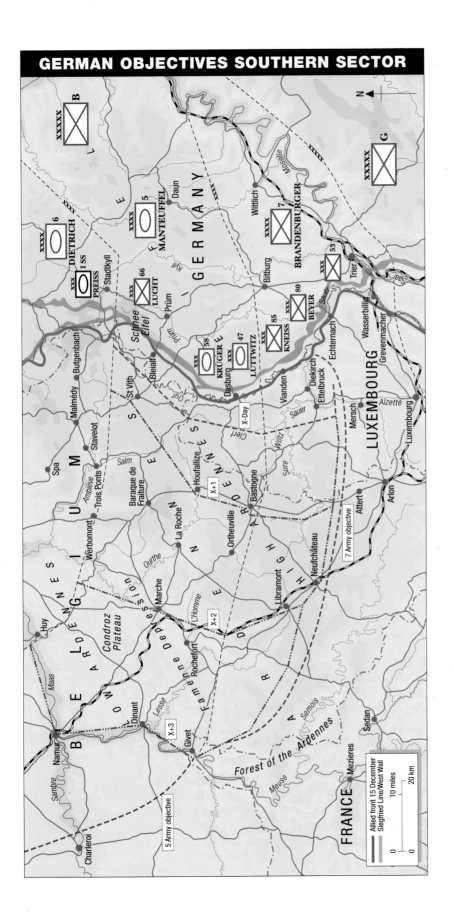

The 7th Army attack was conducted on a narrow axis two corps wide due to the mountainous terrain in Luxembourg. The 85th Infantry Corps on the right was to push through the area around Vianden and, once the US defenses were overcome, swing to the south. The 80th Infantry Corps on the left wing was not expected to push as far through US defenses, but would then swing to the left and establish defensive positions. As in the case of the 5th Panzer Army, the plans contained ambiguous and contradictory elements. Although the emphasis of the plan was for both corps to establish a firm defensive line stretching roughly from Mersch to Gedinne, it also spoke of the need to send out mobile patrols further south along the Semois River to prevent US crossing operations. Yet given the lack of mobility of the divisions under its control, such a task could not be easily accomplished since at many points the Semois was more than 6 miles (10km) further south from the German defensive line.

Hitler ordered a significant shift in Luftwaffe resources to support the Ardennes operation by transferring a large number of fighters from strategic air defense over the Reich to tactical fighter missions over the battlefield. As a result, Luftwaffe Command West's fighter component increased from only 300 single-engine fighters in October 1944 to 1,770 at the time of the offensive. This did not provide much solace for the Wehrmacht however, since there were only 155 ground-attack aircraft available. The majority of fighter pilots were poorly trained compared to their Allied adversaries, and what training they had received focused on ground-controlled intercepts of heavy bombers, not the rough-and-tumble of dogfights and ground strafing. The air operations were supposed to begin with a massive attack on forward Allied airfields codenamed Operation Bodenplatte (baseplate). In the event, the poor weather in the first week of the offensive severely limited Luftwaffe operations and forced the postponement of Bodenplatte until New Year's Day, by which time it was irrelevant. The Ardennes offensive also saw the use of a number of German "wonder weapons", including the bomber version of the Me-262 jet fighter, the first use of the Arado Ar-234 jet bomber, and extensive use of the V-1 guided missile.

The weather in the Ardennes in mid-December was slightly above freezing in the daytime with frequent rain and fog, and sometimes slipping below freezing at night especially in the wooded and hilly areas shaded from the sun. From the German perspective, the frequent overcast and ground fog provided a welcome relief from Allied airpower, and helped to shield the build-up of German forces in the Eifel region. But the weather was a double-edged sword, and the Wehrmacht would pay a price once the offensive began. The wet autumn and frequent cold drizzle left the farm fields in the Ardennes sodden and muddy. This complicated any movement off the roads, and turned every little hamlet and road junction into a bottleneck that had to be overcome before the advance could proceed. For a campaign dependent on speed, the weather was far from ideal.

AMERICAN PLANS

In December 1944, Lieutenant General Omar Bradley's 12th Army Group consisted of three armies. From north to south these were LtGen William H. Simpson's Ninth Army, LtGen Courtney Hodges' First Army and LtGen George S. Patton's Third Army, and they stretched across a front from the Netherlands, along the German–Belgian border to Luxembourg and then to the German frontier along the Saar where they met LtGen Jacob Dever's 6th Army Group. The focus of operations in late November and early December had been on either extreme of the front line, with the central area in the Ardennes quiet due to the difficulty of operating in the hilly and forested terrain. In the northern First and Ninth Armies' zones, the main emphasis had been on the campaign to reach the Roer River, as a preliminary stage to reaching and crossing the Rhine River. By early December, the First Army was in the concluding phase of a bloody struggle to push through the Hürtgen forest to reach the crucial Roer River dams.

The "ghost front" in the Ardennes was held by MajGen Troy Middleton's VIII Corps. The high Ardennes was widely viewed by the US Army as unsuitable for winter operations, so the front was thinly held by four to five divisions. The two northern divisions, the 99th and 106th Divisions, were both green units that had only recently arrived in Europe and were deployed in the quiet Ardennes to gain some experience. The sector further south from St Vith towards Bastogne was held by two veteran divisions, the 28th and 4th Divisions, which had been decimated in the bloody Hürtgen forest fighting. They were in the Ardennes to recuperate and to rebuild their strength. Parts of another new division, the 9th Armored Division, were also present.

Further to the south was Patton's Third Army stretching from Luxembourg into France and posted opposite the Siegfried Line and the Saar region of Germany. Patton's forces had spent November and early December in a series of frustrating battles along the muddy French–German frontier, pushing first through the old Maginot Line then colliding with the Siegfried Line. By mid-December, the Third Army units had secured footholds in the Siegfried Line, and were preparing for a major offensive operation aimed at breaking through the German defensive fortifications and pushing on towards Frankfurt. Codenamed Operation Tink, the attack was planned to be the largest US Army operation of December 1944. Originally scheduled for 19 December, it was finally rescheduled for 21 December.

On 7 December 1944, Eisenhower met with his two senior army group commanders, Bradley and Montgomery in Maastricht to discuss the course of future operations. Montgomery again repeated his view that the 1945 offensive into Germany should be focused on a single thrust spearhead by his 21st Army Group into the northern German plains towards the Ruhr. Eisenhower again disagreed with this strategic option, continuing to favor the broad front approach epitomized by Patton's planned assault towards Frankfurt later in the month. This meeting did not set any specific dates for future offensive operations, since the Allied armies still needed to gain secure footholds for the upcoming Rhine campaign. Little attention was paid to Patton's forthcoming Operation Tink, and it can be surmised that many of the participants felt that it had little more chance of success than the November breakout attempt in the First Army sector, Operation Queen. The presence of the 6th Panzer Army was noted in these discussions, but the general impression was that it was in position near Cologne in preparation for a counter-stroke against any Allied operation over the Rhine.

While most senior Allied leaders failed to anticipate the German offensive in the Ardennes, there were exceptions. One of the most vocal was the G-2 (intelligence) of Patton's Third Army, Colonel Oscar Koch. During a 7 December briefing to Patton in preparation for Operation Tink, Koch detailed the formidable build-up opposite the First Army in the Ardennes, and the potential threat it posed to Third Army operations in the Saar. What worried Patton was the proverbial "dog that did not bark". In spite of some significant advances by Third Army along the Saar in early December, it was not subjected to the usual German counterattack, in spite of the availability of forces along the German frontier. This strongly suggested to him that the Wehrmacht was holding back these units for a specific mission. Patton passed on this assessment to the G-2 section of Eisenhower's headquarters, but when Ike's G-2, General Kenneth Strong, raised this issue with Bradley's intelligence section, they received the standard response. Bradley and his First Army staff were convinced that an offensive in the Ardennes in the winter would be foolhardy, and therefore the force build-up was not for a pre-emptive strike, but rather was intended for a reactive counter-stroke to any major Allied breakthrough towards the Rhine in early 1945.

OPPOSING COMMANDERS

GERMAN COMMANDERS

General der Panzertruppen Erich Brandenberger, commander of the 7th Army in the Ardennes.

The commander of German forces in the west was **Generalfeldmarschall Gerd von Rundstedt**, and the Ardennes sector was the responsibility of Army Group B under **Generalfeldmarschall Walter Model**. Additional details on these senior commanders are contained in the previous volume in this series.[2] The two senior commanders in the southern sector of the Ardennes attack were the two army commanders, Hasso von Manteuffel of 5th Panzer Army and Erich Brandenberger of 7th Army. **General der Panzertruppen Hasso von Manteuffel** was the most talented of the army commanders involved in the Ardennes operation. He was a dynamic, intelligent officer, sometimes nicknamed "Kleiner" by his close friends due to his short stature of only five foot two inches. He was wounded in combat in 1916 while fighting on the Western Front, and had been a youthful advocate of the Panzer force in the 1930s while serving under Heinz Guderian. After a distinguished performance as a regimental commander in North Africa, he was elevated to command the *Grossdeutschland* Division on the Russian Front. He attracted Hitler's personal attention and leapfrogged from divisional commander to 5th Panzer Army commander due to Hitler's favor and his obvious command skills. He was not a political crony like the neighboring 6th Panzer Army commander, Sepp Dietrich, but had received Hitler's recognition as a result of his battlefield accomplishments.

Commander of the 5th Panzer Army, General Hasso von Manteuffel on the left confers with the Army Group B commander, General Walter Model (right) and the inspector of the Panzer force on the Western Front, Generalleutnant Horst Stumpf (center). (MHI)

General der Panzertruppen Erich Brandenberger was a highly capable officer, but his leadership style did not earn him the favor of either Hitler or Model. The Army Group B commander preferred the flashy brilliance of Manteuffel, to the steady, scholarly approach of Brandenberger whom he derided as "a typical product of the general staff system". Yet Brandenberger had a fine combat record, leading the 8th Panzer Division during the invasion of Russia in 1941. He commanded the 29th Army Corps in Russia for a year before the Ardennes offensive when he was given command of the 7th Army.

Manteuffel's corps commanders were, without exception, seasoned Russian Front veterans. They had all started the war as young battalion or regimental commanders and worked their way up through divisional command in Russia. **General der Artillerie Walther Lucht** had begun the war in 1939 as an artillery regiment commander in Poland, and by the time of the France campaign in 1940 he had been elevated to corps artillery command. During the Russian campaign, he was first promoted to army artillery commander, then in February 1942 to command of the 87th Infantry Division, and in March of the 336th Infantry Division, which took part in the efforts to relieve the encircled forces in Stalingrad. He was the area commander for the Kerch Straits in the summer and autumn of 1943 before being posted to 66th Corps command in November 1943 when the formation was on occupation duty in southern France.

General der Panzertruppen Walter Krüger began the war as an infantry regimental commander, was a brigade commander in the 1st Panzer Division during the France campaign in 1940, and was promoted to command the division in July 1941 during the invasion of Russia. He served as the 1st Panzer Division commander in Russia for most of the war, until he was appointed to command the 58th Panzer Corps in February 1944, taking part in the 1944 fighting in France.

General der Panzertruppen Heinrich von Lüttwitz resembled the Hollywood caricature of a German general: fat, monocled, and arrogant.

General der Panzertruppen Heinrich von Lüttwitz, commander of 47th Panzer Corps. (MHI)

Obergruppenführer Willi Bittrich, commander of the II SS-Panzer Corps

Model is seen here consulting with Generalmajor Siegfried von Waldenburg, commander of the 116th Panzer Division in the Ardennes. (MHI)

Generalleutnant Fritz Bayerlein, Rommel's former aide in North Africa, and the commander of Panzer Lehr Division in the Ardennes. (MHI)

Yet he was a seasoned, dynamic Panzer commander. He started the war commanding a motorcycle battalion and became a regimental commander after the France campaign. He first assumed divisional command with the 20th Panzer Division in October 1942, seeing heavy fighting in Russia, and was transferred to the 2nd Panzer Division in February 1944, serving as its commander in the summer fighting in France until the end of August when he was promoted to corps command. The 2nd Panzer Division was the spearhead of his corps during the Ardennes campaign, and he paid it special attention both due to his past connection to the division as well as his doubts about the capabilities of its current commander, Oberst Meinrad von Lauchert who took command only a day before the offensive began.

The corps commanders in Brandenberger's 7th Army were also seasoned Eastern Front veterans, two of them survivors of the summer 1944 debacles in the east. **General der Infanterie Baptist Kneiss** began the war as commander of the 215th Infantry Division, leading it through the early campaigns in France and northern Russia. In November 1942 he was promoted to command the 66th Corps, which was on occupation duty in southern France, and the 85th Corps in July 1944, also in southern France.

General der Infanterie Franz Beyer began the war as an infantry regiment commander, and was promoted to lead the 331st Infantry Division at the end of 1941 during its training in Austria. He remained in command of the division during its assignment to the Russian Front. In March 1943 he was transferred to command the 44th Infantry Division, which was being re-formed in Austria after the original division was lost at Stalingrad and subsequently the unit was deployed to Italy. He was given corps command in late April 1944 on the Eastern Front, serving for short periods with four different corps in the summer battles, finally in the disastrous Crimean campaign in July–August 1944. He was appointed to the 80th Army Corps in early August 1944.

AMERICAN COMMANDERS

The Ardennes sector was part of the front controlled by **Lieutenant General Omar Bradley's** 12th Army Group. The First US Army, commanded by **Lieutenant General Courtney H. Hodges**, covered the broadest area of any Allied army at the time from the Hürtgen forest in the north to the French–Luxembourg border in the south. Hodges was older than Bradley and Patton, and had risen through the ranks of the army after dropping out of the US Military Academy at West Point in 1904 for academic reasons. He saw combat in the Mexican punitive expedition, and again in France in 1918 with the 6th Regiment where he won the Distinguished Service Cross. He was Chief of the Infantry in 1941, and served as deputy commander of the First US Army under Bradley in Normandy in 1944. When the US forces in France expanded in August, Hodges took over command of the First Army when Bradley became 12th Army Group commander. Hodges was the polar opposite to his neighbor to the south, George S. Patton. Dour, reticent, and unassuming, he remained in Bradley's shadow for most of the autumn 1944 campaign. Both Bradley and Eisenhower considered him highly competent, though

ABOVE, LEFT **Major General Troy H. Middleton commanded the VIII Corps in the Bastogne sector and is seen here talking with General Dwight Eisenhower at St Vith in the autumn of 1944. (NARA)**

LEFT **Ike talks with Major General Norman Cota, hero of Omaha Beach, and later commander of the 28th "Keystone" Division during the fighting in the Hürtgen forest and the Ardennes. (NARA)**

ABOVE **George S. Patton awards the Distinguished Service Cross to Brigadier General Anthony McAuliffe on 29 December in Bastogne. McAuliffe was in temporary command of the division during the Battle of the Bulge as Major General Maxwell Taylor was in Washington at the time. (NARA)**

other American commanders felt he was not assertive enough and that he might be overly influenced by his dynamic chief of staff, Major General William Kean. Hodges' performance during the first few days of the campaign remains something of a mystery. Although active in the planning on 16 December when the Germans first attacked, on 17 December he was not widely seen around the headquarters for much of the day. Kean said he was bed-ridden with viral pneumonia for two days. One aide has suggested it was due to nervous exhaustion, and in the event, Kean took over until he recovered.

When command of the US First Army units northwest of Bastogne passed to Montgomery's command, he took control of the counterattack force of VII Corps commanded by Major General J. Lawton Collins to the left and XVIII Airborne Corps led by Major General Matthew Ridgway to the right, seen here at the VII Corps HQ on 26 December. (NARA)

Commander of the US 2nd Armored Division was Major General Ernest Harmon, a classmate of the VII Corps commander, "Lightning Joe" Collins. (NARA)

Although overshadowed by the 101st Airborne Division, the Combat Command B of the 10th Armored Division played a critical role in the initial defense of Bastogne. Here, its commander Colonel W. L. Roberts, is seen after receiving the Silver Star from General Maxwell Taylor in Bastogne after the siege. (MHI)

The southern wing of the Ardennes sector was controlled by VIII Corps, commanded by **Major General Troy H. Middleton**. He was a decade older than many of his German counterparts and had commanded infantry regiments in combat in World War I. The later army chief of staff George Marshall wrote in his file that "this man was the outstanding infantry regimental commander on the battlefield in France." He retired from the Army in 1939 and served as an administrator at Louisiana State University. He returned to the army after war broke out and led the 45th Division in combat on Sicily and during the Italian campaign. He was nearly forced out of the army during the Italian campaign due to knee problems, but his talents were so widely admired that Eisenhower joked that "I'll take him into battle on a litter if we have to." He led the VIII Corps in combat in France in the summer of 1944. At the time of the German attack on 16 December 1944, VIII Corps controlled the sector from St Vith south through Luxembourg, linking with Patton's Third Army near the junction of the French, German, and Luxembourg frontiers.

OPPOSING FORCES

GERMAN UNITS

The Wehrmacht was an emaciated shadow of the force that had conquered most of Europe in 1939–41. The war on the Eastern Front had bled the army white, yet it remained a formidable fighting force and particularly tenacious in its defense of German soil. Its weaknesses became more evident in an offensive operation such as the Ardennes campaign where its lack of motorization, weak logistics, shortage of fuel, and lack of offensive air power severely hampered its striking power.

The fighting power of German infantry divisions had become increasingly illusory as the war progressed due to Hitler's insistence on maintaining a large order of battle. The nominal strength of these units however does not adequately explain their combat potential. The severe personnel shortage in the wake of the 1944 summer debacles forced the Wehrmacht to scrape the bottom of the barrel to recreate the new infantry divisions. Older men, under-age recruits, troops from other services such as the Luftwaffe and navy, and men who had previously been excluded due to medical problems were all put into infantry units, usually with incomplete training. Heavy equipment such as artillery was often an agglomeration of captured foreign types mixed with standard German types. To make matters worse, some of the divisions allotted to the Ardennes offensive had been involved in the furious fighting in the autumn of 1944, and were withdrawn only days or weeks before the start of the offensive without adequate time for rebuilding.

German Panzer regiments in the Ardennes were of mixed composition, including the PzKpfw IV as seen here in the center, and the later Panther Ausf. G seen above and to the right. In the foreground is a SdKfz 251/9 (7.5cm), an assault gun version of the standard German armored half-track used to provide fire support in Panzergrenadier units. (USAOM-APG)

The workhorse of the German field artillery was the 105mm field howitzer like these that were captured by the 35th Division near Lutrebois on 17 January 1945. This is the improved leFH 18/40, which used the lighter carriage of the PaK 40 anti-tank gun. (NARA)

When planning the campaign, Gen Brandenberger of the 7th Army had asked for a Panzer or Panzergrenadier division to spearhead the thrust along 7th Army's right flank plus six infantry divisions. He instead received only four infantry divisions due to the relatively low priority given to this sector. The main effort on the right flank was assigned to the 5th Fallschirmjäger Division, which had been recently rebuilt using only partially trained, surplus Luftwaffe personnel. Brandenburger glumly noted that "In training and in the quality of its officers, both junior and senior, the division displayed notable deficiencies." To make matters worse, many of the senior paratrooper officers were contemptuous and sometimes insubordinate to the new divisional commander. But it was the largest of the divisions in his army, and the best equipped in heavy weapons including an assault gun battalion, so it was given the main mission. The 352nd Volksgrenadier Division was a reconstituted replacement for the division that had fought the US Army so well at Omaha and in Normandy. But it had been badly beaten up in the autumn fighting along the Siegfried Line. It was close to full strength at the start of the offensive, though lacking about a quarter of its authorized NCOs. The 212th Volksgrenadier Division was a reconstruction of a division shattered in Lithuania in the summer of 1944, and rebuilt in Bavaria before the Ardennes campaign. It was closer to authorized strength than the other Volksgrenadier divisions and Brandenberger felt it was his best division. The 276th Volksgrenadier Division was a recreation of a division destroyed in the Falaise pocket in August 1944.

Manteuffel's 5th Panzer Army was significantly larger and with a far better assortment of units due to its more important assignment. The 18th Volksgrenadier Division was created in September 1944 in Denmark using remnants of the 18th Luftwaffe Field Division, surplus navy personnel, and army troops from units shattered on the Eastern Front. It was committed to action near Trier in November, and against the US V Corps during the Roer fighting in early December. It was pulled out of the line shortly before the offensive and brought up to strength. The 62nd Volksgrenadier Division was reconstituted after the disastrous summer 1944 fighting in the east, using inexperienced recruits from the 583rd Volksgrenadier Division.

Heavy firepower for German artillery was provided by the schwere Feldhaubitze 18 15cm. These served in a heavy artillery battalion in German infantry divisions. (MHI)

It was nearly at authorized strength at the start of the offensive but Manteuffel did not consider it suitable for offensive operations.

The 58th Panzer Corps was the weaker of the two Panzer corps in 5th Panzer Army. The 560th Volksgrenadier Division was a new division formed in August 1944 from Luftwaffe personnel in Norway and Denmark and initially deployed in southern Norway. It was near full strength at the start of the offensive, though completely inexperienced. The 116th Panzer Division had been fighting on the Western Front since the summer and had been repeatedly decimated and rebuilt. After taking part in the initial defense of Aachen, the division was withdrawn in the early autumn and rebuilt. Although it was close to authorized strength in personnel at the start of the offensive, it was short of tanks with only 26 PzKpfw IV, 43 PzKpfw V Panthers, and 13 Jagdpanzer IV tank destroyers. At the time, a Panzer division had an authorized strength of 32 PzKpfw IV, 60 PzKpfw V Panthers, and 51 StuG III assault guns. Manteuffel considered all three of his Panzer divisions to be "very suitable for attack" in mid-December even if they were not fully up to strength in armored vehicles.

Lüttwitz's 47th Panzer Corps was the strongest element of Manteuffel's 5th Panzer Army. The 26th Volksgrenadier Division was recreated in October 1944 after its namesake division was decimated by the Red Army along the Baranow front in Poland in September 1944. It was rebuilt with troops from the 582nd VG Division, fleshed out with surplus navy and Luftwaffe troops. The 2nd Panzer Division had been destroyed in the Falaise pocket, and was rebuilt in the Eifel region in the autumn of 1944. It was only slightly better equipped than the 116th Panzer Division, with 26 PzKpfw IV, 49 PzKpfw V Panthers, and 45 StuG III assault guns. The Panzer Lehr Division was destroyed in Normandy during the US breakout

near St Lô, rebuilt again, and sent into action against Patton's Third Army in the Saar. It was pulled out of the front lines at the last moment and deployed to the Ardennes. At the start of the offensive it was close to authorized strength in personnel, but the weakest of Manteuffel's three Panzer divisions in tanks with only 30 PzKpfw IV, 23 PzKpfw V Panthers, and 14 Jagdpanzer IV tank destroyers. The army reserve was the Führer Begleit Brigade, which was relatively well equipped with 23 PzKpfw IV tanks, 20 StuG III assault guns, and a near full complement of troops.

German artillery in the Ardennes was adequate in number, but with feeble motorization and sparse ammunition supplies. In November 1944, the Wehrmacht had only half of the 105mm howitzer ammunition and a third of the 150mm stocks they possessed when attacking Poland in September 1939. After the first few days of the offensive, about half of the towed artillery was left behind by the advancing corps due to lack of motorization and road congestion.

AMERICAN UNITS

One young officer described the Ardennes sector as the US Army's "kindergarten and old-age home" – the sector where the newest and most battle-weary divisions were deployed. The VIII Corps had three infantry divisions and two of the three combat commands of the 9th Armored Division. Its northernmost unit, the 106th Division, was covered in detail in the earlier volume. The 28th Division was deployed along an extended front that largely coincided with the attack sector of the 5th Panzer Army from near the junction of the Belgian–Luxembourg–German borders, south along the Luxembourg frontier. The division was based around a Pennsylvania National Guard division, and was commanded by the hero of Omaha Beach, General Norman Cota. The division had been shattered by the fighting in the Hürtgen forest in early November and had suffered 6,184 casualties in two weeks of fighting, one of the most ferocious blood-

Supplementing the 105mm howitzer in the divisional artillery was the 155mm howitzer. These are from Battery C, 108th Field Artillery Battalion, 28th Division on 11 January near Arsdorf.

The M1 155mm gun was one of the most effective pieces of US field artillery, and was usually deployed in corps-level battalions. This battery is seen in action east of Bastogne on 17 January while supporting Patton's drive to link up with the First Army near Houfallize. (NARA)

lettings suffered by any US Army division in World War II. The division had been sent for rebuilding to the Ardennes front and by mid-December, was back near authorized strength. All three infantry regiments were in the line with the 112th Infantry in the north, the 110th in the center and the 109th in the southern sector. The front was grossly overextended: for example, the 110th held ten miles of front with only two battalions with the third in divisional reserve. Under such circumstances, the best the units could do was to create a thin defensive screen. So typically, the infantry battalions strung out their companies in a few villages a mile or so behind the front on Skyline Drive, the road that ran along the ridgeline that paralleled the frontier. Each company had a few outposts closer to the front that were manned only during daylight hours. With so few forces to cover such a broad front, the regiment was concentrated to bar access to the best routes westward. The heavily forested and hilly front line was in reality a no man's land, and both sides sent out small patrols at night to take prisoners and harass their opponents. Combat Command A of the 9th Armored Division held the area south of the 28th Division. The 9th Armored Division was divided into its three combat commands, with CCA fighting in the south between the 28th and 4th Infantry Divisions, the CCB fighting in the defense of St Vith, and the CCR positioned in reserve. The CCA, 9th Armored Division had a relatively narrow sector about two miles wide along the Our River. Due to its defensive mission, the 60th Armored Infantry Battalion held the front line with the 19th Tank Battalion and 89th Reconnaissance Squadron behind it. The division arrived in Europe in September 1944, but was not committed to action as a whole until the Ardennes fighting.

The 12th Infantry Regiment of the 4th Infantry Division held the southernmost area of the German attack zone. The regiment was spread along a sector about nine miles wide, with the neighboring sector to the south being held by the division's 8th Infantry Regiment. The 4th Infantry Division had landed at Utah Beach on D-Day, and had fought in the brutal hedgerow battles in Normandy through the summer, suffering 100 percent casualties in its infantry companies. The division had recuperated in the early autumn, only to be subjected to the horrific fighting in the Hürtgen forest in November 1944. In two weeks of fighting in late November, the division suffered 6,000 casualties, leaving it a hollow shell. It was deployed on the "ghost front" to recuperate and rebuild. Many of its rifle companies were at half strength, and the attached 70th Tank Battalion had only 11 of its allotted 54 M4 medium tanks. The 12th Infantry, which would bear the brunt of the fighting, had been rated as "a badly decimated and weary regiment" in the days before the German offensive.

ORDER OF BATTLE – SOUTHERN SECTOR, 16 DECEMBER 1944

GERMAN FORCES

5th Panzer Army	**General der Panzertruppen Hasso von Manteuffel**
66th Army Corps	*General der Artillerie Walther Lucht*
18th Volksgrenadier Division	Oberst Günther Hoffmann-Schönborn
62nd Volksgrenadier Division	Oberst Friedrich Kittel
58th Panzer Corps	*General der Panzertruppen Walter Krüger*
560th Volksgrenadier Division	Oberst Rudolf Langhäuser
116th Panzer Division	Generalmajor Siegfried von Waldenburg
47th Panzer Corps	*General der Panzertruppen Heinrich von Lüttwitz*
2nd Panzer Division	Oberst Meinrad von Lauchert
Panzer Lehr Division	Generalleutnant Fritz Bayerlein
26th Volks Grenadier Division	Oberst Heinz Kokott
Reserve	
Führer Begleit Brigade	Oberst Otto Remer
7th Army	**General der Panzertruppen Erich Brandenberger**
85th Army Corps	*General der Infanterie Baptist Kneiss*
5th Fallschirmjäger Division	Generalmajor Ludwig Heilmann
352nd Volksgrenadier Division	Oberst Erich Schmidt

80th Army Corps	*General der Infanterie Franz Beyer*
212th Volksgrenadier Division	Generalleutnant Franz Sensfuss
276th Volksgrenadier Division	Generalmajor Kurt Möhring

AMERICAN FORCES

First US Army	*LtGen Courtney Hodges*
VIII Corps	*MajGen Troy Middleton*
106th Infantry Division	MajGen Alan Jones
28th Infantry Division	MajGen Norman Cota
4th Infantry Division	MajGen Raymond Barton
9th Armored Div. (minus CCB)	MajGen John Leonard

BATTLE OF THE BULGE – SOUTHERN SECTOR

5TH PANZER ARMY VERSUS 28TH DIVISION

The German attack began in the dark, at 05.30hrs on Saturday, 16 December 1944 with a brief 20-minute barrage, 40 rounds per tube, intending to disrupt communication and transport. The barrage succeeded in downing many telephone lines, but could not interfere with radio communication. It was followed by a "fire waltz", a rolling barrage against deeper targets with 60 rounds per tube. The barrage was a mixed blessing for the advancing German infantry, as in many sectors, it did not hit the forward US troop dispositions and merely alerted them to the start of the German attack.

In the pre-dawn hours, shock companies of the German infantry regiments had already begun moving over the front lines in the hopes of infiltrating past the forward American strongpoints before the initial artillery salvoes. These tactics had mixed results. The 116th Panzer Division pushed the shock companies of its two Panzergrenadier regiments forward. One was nearly wiped out by flanking fire from US infantry. The other managed to make its way past the command post of the 1/112th Infantry by dawn but once the sun rose, found itself out in the open and most of its troops were captured. The initial advance of 60th Panzer Regiment went little better, even after some flamethrower tanks were used

A 105mm howitzer of Battery B, 229th Field Artillery Battalion of the 28th Division near Welchenheusen shortly before the start of the Ardennes offensive. (MHI)

to soften up the US infantry machine-gun nests. The only real success on the first day for the 116th Panzer Division occurred at the boundary between the 112th and 110th Infantry when 112th Panzergrenadier Regiment managed to seize a bridge over the Our River near Heiner-scheid. Attempts to seize bridges near Ouren were repeatedly rebuffed by stiff US resistance. The 116th Panzer Division responded the next morning by dispatching 13 Panther tanks to reinforce the Panzergrenadiers. The Panthers advanced right up to the dug-in infantry foxholes, firing point blank. After a frantic radio call, a platoon of M18 76mm gun-motor carriages of the 811th Tank Destroyer Battalion arrived, and managed to knock out four Panzers at a cost of three of their four vehicles. Artillery support from the 229th Field Artillery Battalion proved instrumental in weakening the German attack. One of its forward batteries was brought under direct tank attack, but the accompanying Panzergrenadiers were cut down by a company of M16 anti-aircraft half-tracks, each mounting quadruple .50cal machine-guns. By the afternoon of 17 December, the 116th Panzer Division had committed most of its armor to the fight for Ouren, gradually pushing back the US infantry. By late afternoon, the 112th Infantry was given permission to withdraw to the ridgeline behind Ouren after dark. The 1/112th Infantry, which had been surrounded for most of the day, managed to make their way out by a ruse. On approaching a bridge manned by a few German infantry, the battalion officers lined up the troops in "German formation" and shouting orders in German, marched them across the bridge. The vigorous defense of Ouren forced the 116th Panzer Division to turn their attention south. The 112th Infantry was gradually forced northward, eventually merging its efforts with the defenders of St Vith. In conjunction with the 560th Volksgrenadier Division, the bridgehead at Heinerscheid was reinforced and expanded through 17/18 December, exploiting the gap between the 112th and 110th Infantry.

The hardest hit of the 28th Division's regiments was Colonel Hurley Fuller's 110th Infantry. At a reduced strength of only two battalions, the 110th Infantry was hit by elements of three Panzer divisions and two infantry divisions, roughly 2,000 Americans against 31,000 German troops. The 110th Infantry attempted to hold a string of small villages against the onslaught of the 2nd Panzer Division and Kokott's 26th Volksgrenadier Division on 16 December. Kokott wanted to start the offensive with his forces over the Our River, so he moved two entire regiments over the river prior to the start of the attack. The defenses of the 110th Infantry were so thinly held that this premature deployment was hardly noticed. The west bank of the Our River was soon swarming with Kokott's infantry and Panzergrenadiers from the 2nd Panzer Division. The 110th Infantry clung tenaciously to their village defenses, forcing the Germans to use battalions against single companies, and in some cases, battalions against platoons. The use of Panzers in this sector was delayed by the need to erect a heavy bridge near Dasburg. By late afternoon, the situation in this sector had become so precarious that Cota committed his reserve, the 707th Tank Battalion, in an effort to clear away German infantry who had infiltrated up to the Skyline Drive. The tanks were instrumental in bolstering the infantry defenses and assisting in local counterattacks. By the end of the first day, the situation facing the two forward deployed battalions of the 110th Infantry was grim. They were running low on ammunition, and as darkness

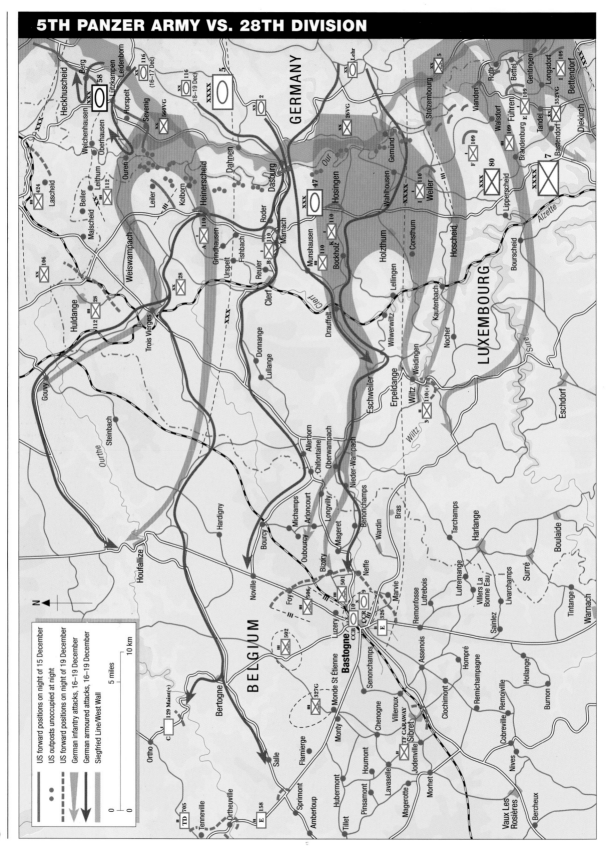

Key:

US forward positions on night of 15 December

US outposts unoccupied at night

US forward positions on night of 19 December

German infantry attacks, 16–19 December

German armoured attacks, 16–19 December

Siegfried Line/West Wall

5 miles

10 km

GERMANY

LUXEMBOURG

BELGIUM

The town of Clerf remains littered with destroyed vehicles in the aftermath of the fighting. To the left is an M4 of the 707th Tank Battalion, which was supporting the 110th Infantry, and to the right is a knocked-out German StuG III assault gun. (NARA)

fell, the German infantry was flowing past them in increasing numbers. Several companies called in artillery on their own positions as they were overrun in the darkness. Two heavy bridges at Dasburg were finished at twilight, and Panzers began moving forward after dark. Although the 48th Panzer Corps had failed to reach its first day objective of the Clerf river, American resistance was obviously weakening as the 110th Infantry was being overwhelmed by forces many times their size. General Cota radioed to the 110th Infantry that they were to hold "at all costs", knowing full well that the regiment guarded the only hard-surface road to Bastogne, the route through Clerf (Clervaux). Cota still had a very modest reserve on hand, 110th Infantry's 2nd Battalion and the light tank company of the 707th Tank Battalion. Before midnight, he ordered the battalion forward to reinforce the Marnach sector in hope of keeping the key road through Clerf blocked to the Panzers.

By dawn on 17 December, German forces were nearing Fuller's headquarters in Clerf. The attempted counterattack by the 2/110th Infantry on the morning of 17 December had hardly set off when it was brought under heavy fire by German infantry supported by Panzers and assault guns. By this stage, the regiment's artillery battalion was down to a single battery, and this unit was driven from its position that morning, losing half its howitzers in the process. The attack by D/707th Tank Battalion went awry when eight of its M5A1 light tanks were picked off by German anti-tank guns, and three more succumbed to anti-tank rockets. A company of infantry made its way into Marnach, only to find that the town had already been abandoned.

With defense of Marnach now impossible, the 110th Regiment attempted to halt the German advance at Clerf. The town was located in a narrow valley with access roads entering down a wooded, winding road. A spearhead from the 2nd Panzer Division consisting of about a dozen PzKpfw IV tanks followed by 30 SdKfz 251 half-tracks full of Panzer-grenadiers, approached the town around 09.30hrs. A platoon of M4 tanks from A/707th Tank Battalion clanked out of town to meet them, and in the ensuing skirmish, the Germans lost four tanks and the American

A pair of survivors of the 110th Infantry, 28th Division on 19 December after the regiment had been shattered by the German assault.

platoon lost three. Diverted from the main road, the German column attempted to enter the town via an alternate road, but this approach was blocked when the lead Panzer was hit. In the meantime, further US reinforcements had arrived in the shape of B/2nd Tank Battalion from 9th Armored Division's CCR. This was not enough to stem the advance, and by nightfall, Clerf was swarming with German tanks and Panzergrenadiers. Around 18.25hrs, Fuller was forced to abandon his headquarters when a German tank stuck its barrel through a window into the command post. Fuller and his headquarters attempted to join up with Company G but were captured. Most of the remnants of the 110th in Clerf withdrew in the darkness, but some US infantry continued to hold out in the stone chateau in the town, sniping at German columns through 18 December as the Panzer columns raced on towards Bastogne.

The 3/110th Infantry had been gradually pushed back out of the border villages by the advance of the 26th Volksgrenadier Division, with the last remnants of the battalion finally congregating in the village of Consthum on 18 December. An afternoon attack, supported by assault guns, penetrated into the town, but fog permitted the American survivors to withdraw out of town, with some 40mm Bofors guns providing a rearguard. The following day, the remnants of the battalion were ordered to withdraw to the divisional headquarters at Wiltz. By the second day of combat, the 110th Infantry had been overwhelmed in their unequal struggle. But their two-day battle had cost the Germans precious time. Middleton later wrote to Fuller, after he was released from a PoW camp, that "had not your boys done the job they did, the 101st Airborne could not have reached Bastogne in time."

The 28th Division's third regiment, the 109th Infantry, was in the attack sector of the German 7th Army. The 5th Fallschirmjäger Division assaulted its northernmost companies on 17 December. The inexperienced Luftwaffe troops did not advance as quickly as their neighbors from 5th Panzer

A patrol of the 28th Division links up with the last GIs to have escaped from Wiltz on 20 December after the town was taken by a combined assault of units of the 5th Panzer Army and 7th Army. (NARA)

Army to the north, but by 18 December, were on their way through the American defenses and approaching the divisional headquarters at Wiltz. By this time, the lead elements of the Panzer Lehr Division had gained access to the roads, and headed towards Wiltz along the northern route. On the morning of 19 December, General Cota transferred the headquarters of the 28th Division from Wiltz to Sibret, leaving behind a provisional battalion formed from the headquarters staff and divisional support personnel, and later reinforced by the 200 survivors of 3/110th Infantry. The commander of the 5th Fallschirmjäger Division, Oberst Heilmann, had planned to bypass Wiltz, but had lost control of his units in the field. In the event, an uncoordinated attack began against Wiltz as the town was near the boundary between the 5th Panzer and 7th Army. Units from the 26th Volksgrenadier Division began an attack from the north on the afternoon of 19 December, while the 15th Parachute Regiment from 5th Fallschirmjäger Division began attacking the town from the south, even though Heilmann had ordered it to attack Sibret. By nightfall, the US defenses had been compressed into the center of the town. The US commander, Colonel Daniel Strickler, decided to retreat, but the withdrawal was confused. The provisional battalion ran a gauntlet of German formations on the way to Bastogne, losing many troops in the process. But some troops did manage to reach Bastogne. The 687th Field Artillery Battalion was surrounded to the south of town, and had to fight off numerous German attacks before a small portion of the unit could withdraw. The 44th Combat Engineers served as the rearguard in Wiltz itself and was decimated in the process.

By 20 December, the 5th Panzer Army had finally overcome the principal centers of resistance held by the 28th Division, and the roads were open towards Houfallize and Bastogne. But the determined defense by the badly outnumbered 28th Division had cost precious time, and by the time that Wiltz was finally taken, Bastogne had already been reinforced. It is worth comparing the performance of the veteran 28th Division against that of the inexperienced regiments of the neighboring 106th Division. While the 106th Division was quickly surrounded and forced to surrender, the battered but experienced regiments of the 28th Division were able to hold off much larger German forces for two days before finally being overwhelmed in desperate combat.

7TH ARMY ATTACKS

Brandenberger's 7th Army had the least ambitious objectives of the three attacking armies, but also had the most modest resources with which to achieve them, and some of the most difficult terrain. The initial artillery barrage that started the offensive was not particularly effective as the 7th Army had poor intelligence on US dispositions. The shock companies leading the attack were generally successful in infiltrating past the forward US outposts due to the huge gaps in the US lines. In Vianden, the 2/109th Infantry outposts in the ruins of the chateau were overrun, but many other outposts were simply bypassed in the early morning fog. Other German assault companies managed to get across the Our River without opposition in rubber boats. The mountainous terrain and the porous defenses permitted the initial German assault battalions to slip through the positions of the 109th Infantry for most of the morning with only sporadic contact with US platoons in the villages. The GR.915 of the 352nd Volksgrenadier Division was able to move most of its forces between the 2nd and 3rd battalions, 109th Infantry, via the deep ravines in the 2,000yd (1,829m) gap between the two battalions. By noon, the 352nd VG Division had scouts well behind the forward US positions, with assault companies not far behind. In contrast, the GR.916 had few terrain advantages, and were quickly pinned down along the Our River by two US artillery battalions that had observers with the 3/109th Infantry on the heights above. By nightfall, the 109th Infantry commander, Colonel James Rudder, thought his situation was reasonably secure except for an encircled company at Führen, not realizing that his positions had been thoroughly penetrated. Around 02.40hrs on 17 December, Rudder was ordered by General Cota to use his reserve to stop an unexpected German penetration. The 14th Parachute Regiment had managed to move some StuG III assault guns and other vehicles across a weir near Vianden, and was motoring down Skyline Drive deep behind American lines from Hosheid towards Ettelbruck. The US garrison in Hosheid was finally forced to withdraw, but their defense held up the paratrooper regiment.

On 17 December, the two German divisions on the right wing of the 7th Army attack continued to move units over the Our River, but their advance was frequently frustrated by small US garrisons, and by accurate artillery fire delivered against their columns from forward observers on the hills above. US attempts to relieve the surrounded company in Führen were frustrated. By late in the day, the vital artillery positions were coming under direct attack as small groups of German troops infiltrated deep behind the forward US positions. Several artillery batteries had to deploy their personnel as riflemen to fight off German infantry. German prospects improved dramatically after nightfall on 17 December when a

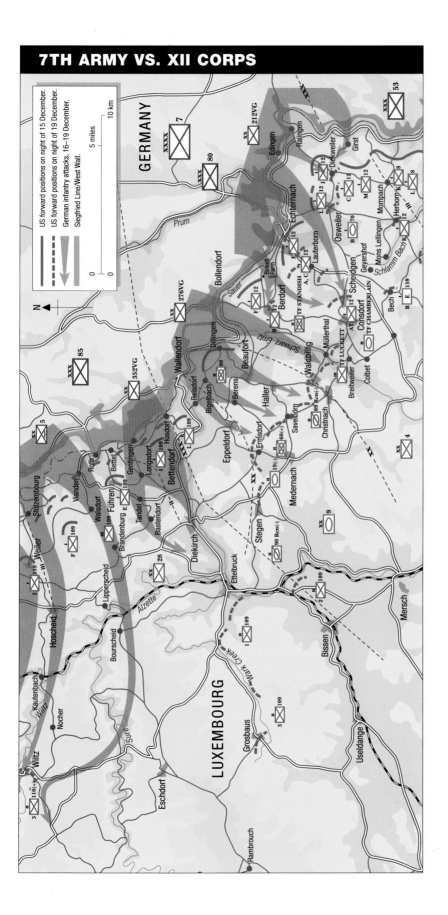

Map legend:
US forward positions on night of 15 December.
US forward positions on night of 19 December.
German infantry attacks, 16–19 December.
Siegfried Line/West Wall.

0   5 miles
0   10 km

N

GERMANY

LUXEMBOURG

long-delayed bridge over the Our was finally completed, permitting the transit of the corps' only armor unit, the 11th Assault Gun Brigade, plus the vehicles and divisional artillery of the 5th Fallschirmjäger Division. The 352nd Volksgrenadier Division's bridge at Gentingen was slow being completed, but by 18 December enough artillery and heavy arms had been moved over the Our that their attack against the 3/109th Infantry intensified considerably. The renewed vigor of the reinforced German attacks on 18 December undermined the 109th Infantry defenses. In the early afternoon, Colonel Rudder received permission to withdraw the regiment back towards the high ground around Diekirch. The 352nd VG Division reached the 109th Infantry defenses around Diekirch on the afternoon of 19 December. The 352nd VG Division had lost so many of its experienced officers and NCOs that in the afternoon the attack was led by the divisional commander, Oberst Erich Schmidt, who was wounded in the process. By the morning of 20 December, the 109th Infantry withdrew to Ettelbruck, destroyed the bridges there, and established defensive positions in the hills west of the town.

A platoon of Co. B, 630th Tank Destroyer Battalion in newly dug foxholes outside Wiltz on the road to Bastogne on 20 December. By this stage, the company had lost all of its 3in. towed anti-tank guns and was assigned by Middleton to defend the approaches to Bastogne. (NARA)

Further to the south, the 7th Army attacks had not progressed as well. The 276th Volksgrenadier Division had crossed the Sauer River opposite the defenses of the 60th Armored Infantry Battalion (AIB) of CCA, 9th Armored Division. Although the division was able to gain a foothold all along the western bank of the river, the three regiments had been unable to overcome the US positions on the high ground. On 17 December, the German infantry managed to infiltrate into the 60th AIB's positions via a deep, wooded gorge. However, the CCA managed to fend off many of the attacks by counterattacking with armored cars of the reconnaissance squadron. After dark, the 1/GR.988 managed to infiltrate behind the 60th AIB and capture the town of Beaufort in spite of a determined stand by a cavalry troop. General Brandenberger was extremely unhappy with the poor performance of the division, and he relieved the commander, even though many of its problems could be traced to the success of American artillery in preventing the construction of a bridge over the Sauer at Wallendorf.

The 60th AIB attempted to rout out the main German incursion by launching a counterattack with the remaining light armored vehicles of the reconnaissance squadron. But when the attack was launched at dawn on 18 December, it stumbled into a battalion of GR.986 that had been reinforced with an anti-tank company with several dozen Panzerschreck and Panzerfaust anti-tank rockets intended for a planned attack towards Medernach. Seven M5A1 light tanks were quickly put out of action, and the cavalry force did not have enough riflemen to contest the German defenses. By the end of the day, the 276th Volksgrenadier Division had made so many penetrations past the forward defenses of CCA, 9th Armored Division, that a new defensive line was established away from the Sauer River. However, the three line companies of the 60th AIB were cut off, and it took three days to extricate the survivors. German attacks slackened on 19 December as the new 276th VG Division commander,

Oberst Dempwolff, attempted to reorganize his demoralized troops, and put off any further attacks until the delayed assault guns finally arrived. When three or four Jagdpanzer 38 finally appeared in the afternoon of 20 December, the GR.988 at Haller launched an attack against a forward US outpost near Waldbillig. The attack failed, but after dark, the GR.987 advanced through a gorge on the other side of Waldbillig forcing the US tank destroyer and cavalry detachments to retreat. Although not apparent at the time, this represented the high-water mark for the division.

The attacks further south by the 212th Volksgrenadier Division against the 12th Infantry, 4th Division, were even less successful. German intelligence in this sector was better and most of the 12th Infantry positions had been accurately spotted. The terrain in this sector was very rugged, the area being known as "Little Switzerland". Two regiments led the German attack over the Sauer River using rubber boats. The main opposition to the crossing proved to be the river itself. Attempts to land the GR.320 near the main objective of Echternach failed due to the swift current, and the regiment had to be landed three miles downstream, delaying the attack. Although radio warnings went out to the widely dispersed 12th Infantry outposts in the early morning, many US units did not receive them, and were unaware of the German attack until German patrols appeared in mid-morning. US artillery was less effective in this sector than further north, even though an artillery observation plane reported that the "area was as full of targets as a pinball machine". Most of the forward US outposts pulled back to the company positions in the forward villages along the frontier, but by late in the day, some of these had been isolated by German infiltration. The 12th Infantry headquarters responded by sending small task groups down the road consisting of a few tanks from the badly under-strength 70th Tank Battalion carrying a small number of infantry reinforcements.

The 5th Fallschirmjäger Division captured six M4 tanks intact in Wiltz, and put them back into service after painting them prominently with German crosses. This one is seen abandoned a few weeks later in the center of Esch-sur-Sûre. (NARA)

By 17 December, the 212th Volksgrenadier Division had managed to reinforce its forward regiments even though its new supply bridge had been knocked down before being completed. While the Germans had significantly more infantry than the 12th Infantry in this sector, the Americans held an advantage in tanks, which was further reinforced on 17 December with a company from the 19th Tank Battalion, 9th Armored Division. In addition, the US forces still had markedly better artillery support since the absence of a bridge had prevented the Germans from bringing any significant artillery across the Sauer. The GR.987 made a deep penetration along the Schwarz Erntz Gorge, but were unable to fight their way out of the gorge after a pummeling by American artillery. Task Force Luckett was formed from some tanks and tank destroyers, and sent towards the gorge to prevent further penetration. The GR.320 had more success by circling around Echternach, thereby penetrating between two rifle companies, but none of these was serious enough to threaten the US defense line.

Breakthrough Achieved

By the morning of 18 December, or X+2 according to the German schedule, the roads to Bastogne were open. The 5th Panzer Army had managed to blast a massive gap in the American lines by overwhelming the 110th Infantry Regiment and pushing back the other regiments of the 28th Division on either side. However, due to the stubborn defense of the 110th Infantry, Hitler's timetable was badly slipping. The plans had called for 5th Panzer Army to take Bastogne on X+1 and reach the Meuse by X+3. The 7th Army's attacks had proceeded less well, particularly in the southernmost area. There were two principal road nets towards the Meuse available to Manteuffel's forces, so the 116th Panzer Division set out via Houfallize while the bulk of the 5th Panzer Army and some elements of the 7th Army headed towards Bastogne.

The delaying actions by the 28th Division gave Middleton some breathing space to prepare the defense of Bastogne. On the afternoon of 16 December, Bradley began to commit his reserves to bolster the badly overextended Ardennes sector. The only reserves available to the 12th Army Group were the 82nd and 101st Airborne Divisions that were refitting near Reims after two months of hard fighting in Holland. The 82nd was directed towards the northern sector around St Vith, and the 101st to the southern sector around Bastogne. With no other reserves on hand, Bradley was forced to pilfer resources from the neighboring armies. Patton's Third Army had the 10th Armored Division in reserve for Operation Tink and Bradley ordered it be sent to Middleton. Patton complained, but when it became evident that the Ardennes attack was no mere spoiling attack, Patton told his staff to reinvigorate plans to reinforce the First Army in the Ardennes.

While waiting for these reinforcements to arrive, Middleton began to deploy the modest reserves he had on hand. Since Bastogne was the most vital initial objective in the corps' area, he was determined to hold it at all costs. Shortly before midnight on 17 December, Middleton learned that Clerf had fallen, giving the 5th Panzer Army access to a good hard road into Bastogne. He planned to block the road using the CCR of the 9th Armored Division. This was reorganized into combined arms teams with mixed companies of infantry and tanks. The weaker of

When the VIII Corps headquarters was ordered to evacuate Bastogne, many corps support units withdrew. This is a column from the 54th Signal Battalion on the road between Bastogne and Marche on 19 December 1944. (MHI)

the two forces, Task Force Rose, was assigned to block the road from Clerf, using a company of tanks and a company of infantry. Task Force Harper was placed behind them near Allerborn, and included less than two companies of tanks and an infantry company. The M7 self-propelled howitzers of the 73rd Armored Field Artillery Battalion (AFAB), near Buret, covered the two task forces. To defend Bastogne itself, Middleton ordered the three engineer battalions of the 1128th Engineer Group to draw weapons and revert to an infantry role, forming a semi-circular defense of Bastogne from Foy in the northeast to Marvie in the south.

The first contact between the advancing 5th Panzer Army and the Bastogne defenders occurred at 08.30hrs, when reconnaissance elements of the 2nd Panzer Division encountered Task Force Rose at the Lullange roadblock. The remainder of the division was delayed due to continued sniper fire from Americans still holding out in Clerf. After inconclusive skirmishing early in the morning, the lead Kampfgruppe laid smoke in front of the American positions, and moved two companies of Panzers forward under its cover. When the smoke lifted around 11.00hrs, tank fighting ensued at ranges of around 800 yards (732m) with both sides losing three tanks. The Kampfgruppe deployed forces on all three sides of the roadblock and gradually whittled it away. Permission was requested to pull back TF Rose or reinforce it from TF Harper, but Middleton refused both requests. The situation deteriorated in the early afternoon when elements of the advancing 116th Panzer Division brushed up against the 73rd AFAB in Buret, forcing them to redeploy. In the early evening, TF Rose was given permission to pull back a few miles to Wincrange, in part to deal with Panzers that had been leaking past the Lullange roadblock. By the time it had pulled back, it was completely surrounded by advancing elements of the 2nd Panzer Division and cut off from TF Harper.

The TF Harper roadblock at Allerborn was hit by artillery around 20.00hrs followed closely by a Panzer attack. The 9th Armored Division accounts claim that the attack was so successful due to the use of infrared.

night-fighting equipment on the Panthers but there is no evidence that this was actually the case. By midnight, TF Harper had been shattered. The commander and assault gun platoon escaped northward towards Houfallize, and the other battalion vehicles southward towards Tintigny. This left only some token headquarters units, two self-propelled artillery battalions, and a platoon of light tanks along the road into Bastogne. With its forces destroyed or surrounded, the headquarters elements of the CCR, 9th Armored Division, began pulling back to Bastogne shortly after midnight.

Combat Command B, 10th Armored Division, drove from Arlon to Bastogne on 18 December and was instructed by Middleton to divide into three teams to cover Longvilly, Wardin, and Noville. Team Cherry arrived in Longvilly on the night of 18 December, but was instructed to advance no further in spite of the predicament of TF Harper. The plans to use CCB, 10th Armored Division, to defend this corridor quickly went awry.

The unit assigned to take Bastogne was Bayerlein's Panzer Lehr Division. On 18 December, it was split into two Kampfgruppen based around its two Panzergrenadier regiments, Kampfgruppe Poschinger (Panzergrenadier Regt.902) on the road behind the southern wing of 2nd Panzer Division heading towards Oberwampach, and Kampfgruppe Hauser (Panzergrenadier Regt.901), still engaged with the 3/110th Infantry at Consthum. With Panzer Lehr in action east of Bastogne, the 2nd Panzer Div. Kampfgruppe that had attacked TF Cherry and TF Harper veered off northward towards Noville in an effort to reach the Meuse river. Delayed by the muddy road conditions, KG Poschinger reached Oberwampach around 18.30hrs on the evening of 18 December, and penetrated into Mageret after midnight. But the Panzers were without infantry support since the Panzergrenadiers and their Steyr trucks were stuck in the muddy roads leading to the town. There, Bayerlein encountered a Belgian civilian who told him, erroneously, that at least 40 American tanks and many more vehicles, led by an American two-star general had passed through Mageret that evening. At the time, Bayerlein had less than a dozen of his tanks with him, and was concerned that he had stumbled into a US armored division. He ordered a defensive deployment on the northeast side of Mageret and decided to wait until morning to launch his attack towards Bastogne.

The lead elements of the 101st Airborne Division arrived in Bastogne by truck on the night of 18 December. The division was led by Brigadier General Anthony McAuliffe, the divisional artillery officer, as its commander, Maxwell Taylor was back in the US. The division had little time to prepare for the move, and the troops left without adequate cold weather uniforms or ammunition. In view of the increasingly precarious situation around Bastogne, Bradley ordered Middleton to pull his corps headquarters out of the city on 19 December and leave command of Bastogne to McAuliffe. Julian Ewell's 501st Parachute Infantry Regiment (PIR) was the first into Bastogne, and deployed a combat team from 3rd Bn, 501st PIR to try to determine the situation along the road to Mageret.

Increasingly skittish due to the sudden appearance of more and more new American units, Bayerlein ordered his advance guard, Kampfgruppe Fallois, to push through Neffe in the hope that a fast raid might gain a foothold in the outskirts of Bastogne. Neffe was held by the headquarters

of Team Cherry and a few tanks. Although KG Fallois was able to push into Neffe by 08.00hrs, they had not thoroughly cleared the town of American troops, and had overlooked American infantry in the stone chateau. On reaching the edge of the town and peering towards Bastogne they saw columns of American infantry advancing forward, a glimpse of Ewell's combat team. The paratroopers were supported by an air-portable 105mm light howitzer, the sound of which Bayerlein misinterpreted as tank fire. Instead of raiding into Bastogne, Bayerlein ordered his forces in this sector to prepare to repulse what he thought was a major American counterattack and not merely a local probe. The pugnacious sally by the paratroopers derailed Bayerlein's long delayed attack into Bastogne. Furthermore, Panzergrenadiers marching through Neffe were dispersed by sniper fire from US troops still in the castle, and even tank gun fire could not get them to budge.

Even though Team Cherry was surrounded in Longvilly, it posed a threat to the planned attack of the 26th VG Division towards Bizory, so Bayerlein decided to clean it out once and for all. In the meantime, the division's second Kampfgruppe had been freed of its assignment near Consthum, and lead elements including the divisional tank destroyer battalion, Panzerjäger Lehr Abteilung 130, arrived that morning. The attack on Longvilly began hours late, in the early afternoon. As the tank destroyers crested the ridge of Hill 490, they encountered an enormous traffic jam of US vehicles consisting of advancing elements of CCB, 10th Armored Div., retreating elements of CCR, 9th Armored Div., and various and sundry other US units. Besides the Panzer Lehr Kampfgruppe, the 26th VG Division was also closing in on this area, and the 2nd Panzer Division had sent six 88mm tank destroyers to deal with 9th Armored Division self-propelled howitzers that had been shelling their troops. Elements of these three German divisions began to descend on the trapped American column, systematically destroying it. Team Cherry tried to get off the road and defend the area, but lost all 14 of its medium and

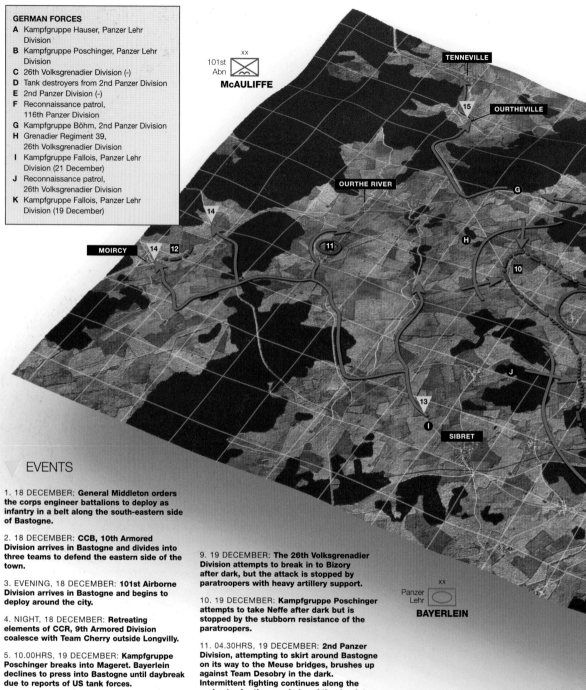

GERMAN FORCES

A Kampfgruppe Hauser, Panzer Lehr Division
B Kampfgruppe Poschinger, Panzer Lehr Division
C 26th Volksgrenadier Division (-)
D Tank destroyers from 2nd Panzer Division
E 2nd Panzer Division (-)
F Reconnaissance patrol, 116th Panzer Division
G Kampfgruppe Böhm, 2nd Panzer Division
H Grenadier Regiment 39, 26th Volksgrenadier Division
I Kampfgruppe Fallois, Panzer Lehr Division (21 December)
J Reconnaissance patrol, 26th Volksgrenadier Division
K Kampfgruppe Fallois, Panzer Lehr Division (19 December)

101st Abn **XX** **McAULIFFE**

TENNEVILLE

OURTHEVILLE

OURTHE RIVER

MOIRCY

SIBRET

Panzer Lehr **XX** **BAYERLEIN**

▼ EVENTS

1. 18 DECEMBER: **General Middleton orders the corps engineer battalions to deploy as infantry in a belt along the south-eastern side of Bastogne.**

2. 18 DECEMBER: **CCB, 10th Armored Division arrives in Bastogne and divides into three teams to defend the eastern side of the town.**

3. EVENING, 18 DECEMBER: **101st Airborne Division arrives in Bastogne and begins to deploy around the city.**

4. NIGHT, 18 DECEMBER: **Retreating elements of CCR, 9th Armored Division coalesce with Team Cherry outside Longvilly.**

5. 10.00HRS, 19 DECEMBER: **Kampfgruppe Poschinger breaks into Mageret. Bayerlein declines to press into Bastogne until daybreak due to reports of US tank forces.**

6. 08.30HRS, 19 DECEMBER: **Kampfgruppe Fallois pushes into Neffe, but spots an approaching patrol from the 3/501st Parachute Infantry Regiment.**

7. EARLY AFTERNOON, 19 DECEMBER: **A trapped column consisting of elements of the CCR, 9th Armored Division and Team Cherry, 10th Armored Division are attacked and destroyed by elements from three German divisions.**

8. **Team O-Hara is attacked by Kampfgruppe Fallois, Panzer Lehr Division, which pushes them out of Wardin and back towards Marvie.**

9. 19 DECEMBER: **The 26th Volksgrenadier Division attempts to break in to Bizory after dark, but the attack is stopped by paratroopers with heavy artillery support.**

10. 19 DECEMBER: **Kampfgruppe Poschinger attempts to take Neffe after dark but is stopped by the stubborn resistance of the paratroopers.**

11. 04.30HRS, 19 DECEMBER: **2nd Panzer Division, attempting to skirt around Bastogne on its way to the Meuse bridges, brushes up against Team Desobry in the dark. Intermittent fighting continues along the perimeter for the remainder of the day, intensifying with the arrival of the 1/506th PIR.**

12. 05.30HRS, 20 DECEMBER: **Starting with a pre-dawn attack, 2nd Panzer Division pushes Team Desobry back from Noville and breaks into the paratrooper defenses in Foy.**

13. 21 DECEMBER: **As it becomes evident that the defense of Bastogne has hardened, Luttwitz gives Bayerlein permission to move the Panzer Lehr Division around the south side of Bastogne to continue its race for the Meuse bridges. With Kampfgruppe Fallois in the lead, this move will cut off Bastogne from the south and west.**

14. 21 DECEMBER: **Late in the day Kampfgruppe Fallois reaches the Ourthe river crossings.**

15. 20 DECEMBER: **Kampfgruppe Böhm, the reconnaissance element of the 2nd Panzer Division, seizes a bridge over the Ourthe river at Ortheuville. Kampfgruppe Cochenhausen follows, but the division is unable to quickly exploit the breakthrough due to a lack of fuel.**

42

BASTOGNE ENCIRCLED

19–23 December 1944, viewed from the southeast. Spearheads of the 5th Panzer Army reach the outskirts of Bastogne in the pre-dawn hours of 19 December. They are thwarted in their attempts to capture the city on the run by the sacrifice of several armored task forces on the approach roads to the city, and by the timely arrival of the 101st Airborne Division. As a result, the 2nd Panzer Division and Panzer Lehr Division bypass the city to reach their main objective of the Meuse River crossings. By 21 December Bastogne is cut off.

Note gridlines are shown at intervals of 1 mile/1.61km

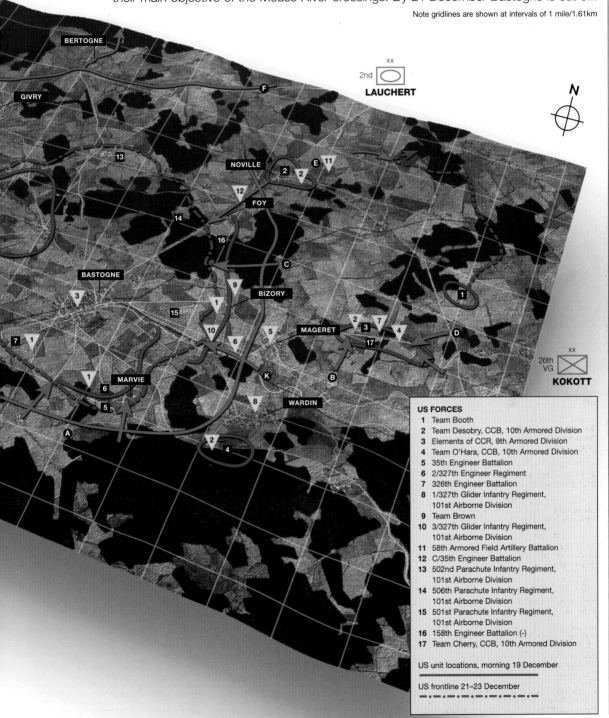

US FORCES
1 Team Booth
2 Team Desobry, CCB, 10th Armored Division
3 Elements of CCR, 9th Armored Division
4 Team O'Hara, CCB, 10th Armored Division
5 35th Engineer Battalion
6 2/327th Engineer Regiment
7 326th Engineer Battalion
8 1/327th Glider Infantry Regiment,
   101st Airborne Division
9 Team Brown
10 3/327th Glider Infantry Regiment,
   101st Airborne Division
11 58th Armored Field Artillery Battalion
12 C/35th Engineer Battalion
13 502nd Parachute Infantry Regiment,
   101st Airborne Division
14 506th Parachute Infantry Regiment,
   101st Airborne Division
15 501st Parachute Infantry Regiment,
   101st Airborne Division
16 158th Engineer Battalion (-)
17 Team Cherry, CCB, 10th Armored Division

US unit locations, morning 19 December

US frontline 21–23 December

Although the 116th Panzer Division managed to break into Hotton, they were pushed out by headquarters elements of the 3rd Armored Division. This is a PzKpfw IV tank of II/Panzer Regiment 16 knocked out during the fighting on the afternoon of 21 December. (NARA)

Two tanks helped buttress the US defense of Hotton on 21 December and this M4 of Co. G, 33rd Armored Regiment was knocked out in the fighting. (NARA)

light tanks in the process. In all, about 100 US vehicles were abandoned or destroyed, including 23 M5A1 and M4 tanks, 15 M7 105mm self-propelled howitzers, 14 armored cars, 30 jeeps and 25 2$^{1}/_{2}$ ton trucks. The destruction of this trapped column distracted the lead elements of the Panzer Lehr Division from their main assignment of Bastogne.

The next element from the CCB, 10th Armored Division, to encounter Panzer Lehr was Team O'Hara, located near Wardin, covering the south-eastern approach to Bastogne. An attack by KG Fallois pushed them out of Wardin and back towards Marvie on the afternoon of 19 December, but further German attacks were stymied.

On the afternoon of 19 December, the corps commander, General Lüttwitz, visited Bayerlein to discuss the best approach to dealing with Bastogne. Lüttwitz was extremely agitated by the number of new US units showing up in Bastogne, and feared that if the corps did not race to the Meuse now and bypass Bastogne, that the Americans would soon receive more reinforcements. Bayerlein argued that Bastogne was indispensable to any future operations and that it would continue to pose a threat even if bypassed. Bayerlein ordered a night attack by Kampfgruppe Poschinger from Neffe starting at 19.00hrs, which would coincide with a similar advance by the 26th VG Division towards Bizory. Neither attack proved fruitful and both encountered growing resistance. The outer defenses of Bastogne had been soft and relatively easy to penetrate; now they had hit a solid defense line.

While Panzer Lehr and the 26th VG Division were conducting their fruitless attacks on the southeastern edge of Bastogne, the 2nd Panzer Division had raced to the northeast outskirts with the intention of heading west. Around 04.30hrs, reconnaissance units had discovered the outer perimeter of Team Desobry, the third of the CCB, 10th Armored Division, outposts. Lauchert radioed to Lüttwitz to get permission to bypass the roadblocks near Bourcy and Noville in order to head west to the Meuse River, and the corps commander agreed. The German armored columns advanced in the fog, one of the columns moving across a ridge southeast of Noville. The fog occasionally lifted, leading to sharp, close-range duels between the Panzers and the US tanks. Realizing he was seriously outgunned, Desobry asked for permission to withdraw. This was denied as the 101st Airborne needed time to get its rifle companies into the line. When paratroopers of the 1/506th PIR arrived in the early afternoon, the aggressive paratroopers staged a counterattack, but it was quickly suppressed by tank fire. The 2nd Panzer Division responded with an infantry attack backed by two companies of tanks, but the German Panzers wisely decided to avoid tangling with the paratroopers and their bazookas in the ruins of Noville. The town could not be easily bypassed since the fields were too muddy to support the trucks following the lead Panzer columns. The attacks resumed at 05.30hrs on the morning of 20 December, cutting off Noville and pushing the paratroopers out of neighboring Foy. McAuliffe recognized that the Noville force stood no chance, and so gave permission for them to withdraw while other paratroopers tried to retake Foy. The column started to move out around dusk and, to their good fortune, fog settled, which hid their movement from surrounding German troops. The 2nd Panzer Division continued its race east, and captured a bridge over the Ourthe River near Ourtheville. But the lead columns were so short of fuel that they had to wait nearly a day for supplies to catch up.

Bayerlein resumed his attempts to crack through the Bastogne defenses near Bizory on the morning of 20 December. Small arms fire and artillery put an end to the Panzer Lehr attack, forcing Bayerlein to look elsewhere. Kampfgruppe Poschinger and infantry from the 26th VG Division attempted to fight their way further south, near Neffe, but a strong response from US artillery broke up several attacks. By 21 December, it was becoming obvious that Panzer Lehr Division was being wasted in costly attacks against the Bastogne defenses. The 2nd Panzer Division had already skirted around Bastogne to the north, and finally Lüttwitz gave Bayerlein permission to try the same to the south. But KG Hauser was left behind to reinforce the attacks by the 26th VG Div., thereby significantly weakening the division's attempt to reach the Meuse. The Panzer Lehr Division, with KG Fallois in the lead, set out for the Ourthe River near St Hubert on 22 December. In combination with the 2nd Panzer Division's advance to the Ourthe the preceding day, this left Bastogne surrounded.

While Manteuffel focused most of his attention on the Bastogne sector, Krüger's 58th Panzer Corps had encountered prolonged delays in executing its breakthrough on the Tailles plateau. Although the 112th Infantry had been pushed northward after three days of fighting, the 116th Panzer Division, had been very slow to exploit the rupture in the American lines. Poor bridges, traffic jams and the ensuing lack of fuel proved as nettlesome as the US Army. Manteuffel was so upset that on 19 December, he told Krüger he was thinking of relieving the divisional commander. His attitude changed during the day as the fortunes of the division abruptly improved. US defenses in the area around Houfallize were extremely thin, as units were tending to coalesce around St Vith to the north and Bastogne to the south. In the early morning, the divisional reconnaissance reported that Houfallize was not occupied by US forces and that the bridges were intact. The divisional commander, General von Waldenburg, decided to bypass Houfallize to the south, and the division reached Bertogne and the main road from Marche to Bastogne by evening. Indeed US resistance was so weak, that even the unmotorized 560th VG Div. was making good progress, passing by Houfallize to the north. Now the concern was no longer the corps' slow advance, but the open flank to the south as the 58th Panzer Corps outpaced its southern neighbor, Lüttwitz's 47th Panzer Corps around Bastogne. One of the unit officers recorded that "the Americans are completely surprised and in substantial turmoil. Long columns of prisoners march toward the east, many tanks were destroyed or captured. Our *Landsers* are loaded with cigarettes, chocolates, and canned food, and are smiling from ear to ear."

Reassessing the Plans

On 18 December, Patton met with Bradley at his Luxembourg headquarters. When asked what the Third Army could do to help the First Army in the Ardennes, Patton asserted that he could have two more divisions on the move the following day and a third in 24 hours. Patton was not happy to give up Operation Tink, but he ruefully remarked "What the hell, we'll still be killing Krauts." Unwilling to gloat in view of Bradley's anguish, Patton did not mention that his ability to shift a corps into the Ardennes was precisely because his staff had anticipated the German attack and had already prepared a set of contingency plans, while Bradley's had failed him. The following day, Eisenhower held a conference of all the senior US commanders in Verdun. The atmosphere was glum except for Patton who was his usual cocky self.

US Army doctrine suggested that the essential ingredient to countering an enemy offensive was to hold the shoulders. This objective seemed to be well in hand. Units on the northern shoulder on the Elsenborn Ridge had rebuffed every German assault, and the battered 4th Division was holding steady in the hills of Luxembourg. Eisenhower's short-term objective was to prevent the Germans from crossing the Meuse. Once forces were in place to hold the river line, Eisenhower wanted to begin a counter-offensive, and he turned to Patton asking him when he could start. Patton promptly replied that he could begin with a corps of three divisions within two days, on the morning of 21 December, to which Eisenhower blurted "Don't be fatuous, George", thinking that it was merely Patton's usual bluster. The other officers present were equally skeptical, recognizing the enormous difficulties of reorienting a corps 90 degrees, moving it in winter conditions, and keeping it supplied along a tenuous supply line. In the ensuing discussion, Patton made it quite clear that his plans had been well considered. Eisenhower, who had just received his fifth star, quipped to Patton: "Funny thing, George, but every time I get a new star, I get attacked." Patton smiled and responded, "And every time you get attacked Ike, I pull you out", referring to his role in redeeming the US Army after the Kasserine Pass debacle in 1943.

Patton's actual dream for this campaign would have been to allow the Germans to penetrate 40 or 50 miles (60–80km), and then cut them off in an envelopment operation. But he realized that the senior US commanders were too cautious for such a bold plan, especially under the present confused circumstances. Curiously enough, Patton's notion of a deep envelopment battle was the worst nightmare of the senior Wehrmacht commanders. Model was concerned that the US Army would wait until after the Wehrmacht had reached or even crossed the Meuse before launching a major counter-offensive, trapping most of Army Group B and ending the war in the West.

On 20 December, under pressure from his senior aides, Eisenhower decided to temporarily shift control of the elements of the US Army in the northern sector, including First and Ninth Army, from Bradley's 12th Army Group to Montgomery's 21st Army Group. The ostensible reason was the fear that the Germans were about to capture a vital communications

A tank patrol of the 3rd Armored Division scans for signs of the 116th Panzer Division near Houfallize on 23 December. The tank to the left is an M4A1 (76mm) while the one to the right is an M4A3E2 assault tank. (NARA)

junction that would have severed the landlines between Bradley's HQ in Luxembourg and the northern commands. But there were also concerns that the First Army staff was still in disarray and that Bradley had not been vigorous enough straightening out the problems. The switch caused enormous resentment due to past problems between Bradley and Montgomery in North Africa and Sicily, and Montgomery's persistent efforts to poach units from Bradley to reinforce his infantry-weak 21st Army Group. The short-term effects were beneficial, and Montgomery's take-charge style impressed American officers fighting in the St Vith salient. In the long term, the switch in command would prove to be troublesome due to Montgomery's maladroit control of the US corps.

Montgomery showed up at First Army HQ in Chaudfontaine on the afternoon of 20 December "like Christ come to cleanse the temple". After Hodges explained the current dispositions, Montgomery responded that he wanted to redeploy the forces, create a reserve, and use this reserve to counterattack once the German attack had run out of steam. The US officers strongly resisted giving up any ground, and wanted to begin counter-offensive operations immediately. Montgomery accepted the current dispositions, and ordered the transfer of Collins' VII Corps, which would form the northern counterattack force, from the idle Ninth Army sector. British officers on Montgomery's staff thought that Hodges looked like he had "been poleaxed" but when Montgomery tried to relieve him the following day, Eisenhower told him to be patient. The matter was dropped, but Hodges' performance over the next few weeks was underwhelming and the First Army staff depended heavily on his chief of staff, MajGen William Kean.

The mobilization of the two heavy armored divisions, the 2nd and 3rd Armored, stationed north of the Ardennes was already under way, and these were assigned to Collins' corps. Since the 3rd Armored Division was more easily redeployed than the 2nd, on 18 December its CCA was detached and sent to V Corps, taking part in the fighting against the spearhead of the 1st SS-Panzer Division, Kampfgruppe Peiper, near La Gleize in the northern sector. The remainder of the division arrived around Hotton on 20 December. The two heavy divisions followed the old 1942 tables of organization and had six tank battalions instead of the three found in all other US armored divisions. The divisions were tank-heavy and infantry-weak, so they were usually paired with infantry divisions for a more balanced force with an infantry regiment added to

An armored dough of the 3rd Armored Division mans a roadblock with a bazooka near Manhay on 23 December, hours before the 2nd SS-Panzer Division attack. (NARA)

A Panther Ausf. G of 2nd SS-Panzer Division knocked out in a fork in the road between Manhay and Grandmenil during the fighting on 23 December 1944 with the 3rd Armored Division.

49

When the advance guard of Panzer Lehr Division pushed into Neffe in the pre-dawn hours of 19 December, the lead Panther tank of Feldwebel Dette struck a mine, blocking the road and ending the initial attack. This shows Dette's tank later in the month after it had been pushed off the road during subsequent attacks. (MHI)

each of their three combat commands. Collins' VII Corps deployed two infantry divisions, the green 75th Division and the more experienced 84th Division, in this role.

On the evening of 18 December 1944, a series of telephone conversations were held between the senior Wehrmacht commanders. In separate conversations with Rundstedt and Jodl, Army Group B commander Walter Model told them that the offensive had failed due to the inability of the SS divisions to move forward, and the slow progress of Manteuffel's 5th Panzer Army. He indicated that not only were the "Grand Slam" objectives out of reach, but that he doubted that even "Little Slam" could be achieved since the Panzer spearheads were so far from the Meuse. This sentiment gradually permeated the various headquarters in Berlin, and on 20 December 1944, when Heinz Guderian visited Hitler's HQ and the OB West offices, he tried to pry away some of the prized Panzer divisions in the Ardennes to reinforce threatened sectors on the Russian Front. Hitler would not hear of such a thing and scorned the generals for their pessimism. Due to the dissension in the high command as well as difficulties in moving reserve units forward, Model was slow to reorient the focus of the offensive. Even Dietrich and the 6th Panzer Army staff understood the problems, and on 20 December suggested to Model that either all the Panzer divisions be directed towards Dinant to exploit the breakthrough of the 2nd Panzer Division, or alternately to reorient their own attack away from the stubborn Elsenborn Ridge, towards the central route being spearheaded by 116th Panzer Division, Houfallize–La Roche–Liege.

At noon on 20 December, the II SS-Panzer Corps was ordered to begin moving forward. Since there was still a slim hope that I SS-Panzer Corps might secure a breakthrough in the northern sector, no decision was made whether its SS-Panzer divisions would be committed to the 6th Panzer Army as planned, or shifted to exploit the successes of Manteuffel's 5th Panzer Army. Manteuffel later argued that it was this indecision in these critical few days that prevented the success of "Little Slam", since an early commitment of the several Panzer divisions in reserve could have provided the added impetus needed to push to the Meuse. But Model recognized that until the American salient at St Vith was eliminated, there was no maneuver room to shift the SS-Panzer divisions into the central sector. The German appreciation actually became more optimistic in the days before Christmas. The OB West intelligence briefing of 22 December asserted that a major Allied counterattack by the US Third or Seventh Army from the south was unlikely before the New Year, and that limited intervention along the flanks would probably not start for a week. In conjunction with the reduction of the American salient at St Vith, the German high command began to take steps to redeploy the II SS-Panzer Corps away from the northern sector and into the center where it could support the penetration by the 5th Panzer Army.

The stage was now set for some of the largest and most bitter battles of the Ardennes campaign. The fighting through Christmas in the southern sector was concentrated in three main areas: Bastogne, the approaches to the Meuse River near Dinant, and the road junctions along the Tailles plateau beyond Houfallize.

THE DEFENSE OF BASTOGNE

The decision to free Panzer Lehr Division to race for the Meuse reduced the strength of the German forces around Bastogne. Although Lüttwitz had ordered Bayerlein to leave Kampfgruppe Hauser behind to reinforce Kokott's 26th VG Div., this meant that the attack was only being conducted by a reinforced division. Even after two days of futile fighting to penetrate into Bastogne, Kokott had not lost hope. When he accompanied a reconnaissance battalion in a move towards Sibret, he continued to see evidence of US troops retreating out of the city towards the south, an area not yet firmly in German hands. If he could not break into Bastogne, at least he could choke it. From 20 to 22 December, Kokott continued to draw the cordon around Bastogne with GR.77 on the north and east side, Kampfgruppe Hauser the southeast and GR.39 the southern flank around Sibret. Even though his forces did not yet firmly control the western side of Bastogne, word from the neighboring corps was that the 5th Fallschirmjäger Div. was making good progress, and so would presumably take care of this sector.

When the road to Neufchateau was cut on the night of 20 December, Bastogne was effectively surrounded, even if the Germans did not control the western sector in any force. Until that point, command within the city was disjointed, with Colonel Roberts controlling CCB, 10th Armored Div., General McAuliffe commanding the 101st Airborne, with a number of separate corps units and groups of stragglers. Middleton decided that it was time to unify the command in Bastogne and so it was turned over to McAuliffe. The scattered stragglers were formed into Team SNAFU, a GI jibe against the fondness of the Army for acronyms, meaning "Situation Normal All F'ed Up". Team SNAFU was broken up into security patrols and used where needed around the city. The German repositioning on 21/22 December gave McAuliffe time to better organize the defenses.

At 11.30hrs on 22 December, two Panzer Lehr officers and their drivers walked up the road from Remonfosse under a white flag. Under

Lüttwitz's direction, they were to offer the Bastogne defenders an honorable surrender. They encountered an outpost of the 327th Glider Infantry and the officers were taken to McAuliffe's HQ in blindfolds. When told of the surrender demands, McAuliffe laughed and said "Aw, nuts". The idea of surrendering seemed preposterous to him as the Germans had proven unable to break into the city after four days of fighting. McAuliffe was at a loss as to how to reply to the formal surrender demand, however, until one of his staff suggested that his first reaction was fine. So they typed out "Nuts" on some stationery, thereby creating one of the legends of the Ardennes campaign. When the response was handed over to the German officers before they returned

LEFT **Newly arrived paratroopers of Ewell's 501st Parachute Infantry Regiment, 101st Airborne Division, head out of Bastogne towards Mageret on the morning of 19 December. It was the appearance of this column that dissuaded Bayerlein from launching a raid by Panzer Lehr Division into Bastogne that day. (NARA)**

BELOW **Paratroopers of the 1/506th PIR, 101st Airborne Division, set off from Bastogne for Foy in the late morning of 19 December to reinforce Team Desobry near Noville. (NARA)**

to Lüttwitz, they expressed puzzlement at the answer, to which the 327th Glider Infantry commander, Colonel Harper responded "If you don't understand what 'Nuts' means in English it is the same as 'go to hell', and I'll tell you something else – if you continue to attack we will kill every goddam German that tries to break into this city."

The success of the Bastogne garrison in repulsing repeated German infantry attacks was closely tied to the field artillery battalions that had accumulated within the Bastogne perimeter. But ammunition reserves were becoming dangerously low by the evening of 22 December. This led to restrictive instructions on the use of the howitzers, frustrating the

Surviving troops of the 28th Division and stragglers from other units were used to form Team SNAFU to conduct security patrols around Bastogne like this 28th Division patrol on 20 December. (NARA)

A view inside Bastogne on 26 December shortly before the relief column from the 4th Armored Division arrived. In the background is an M4A3 tank, probably of the 10th Armored Division.

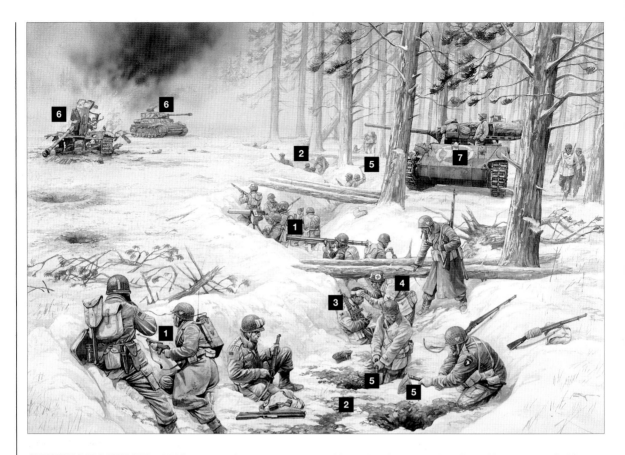

CHRISTMAS IN BASTOGNE, 1944 (pages 54–55)

In the early morning of Christmas Day, Kampfgruppe Maucke of the newly arrived 15th Panzergrenadier Division launched an attack against the positions of the 502nd Parachute Infantry (1) and the 327th Glider Infantry on the northern side of the Bastogne perimeter. The attack was beaten decisively in a series of savage skirmishes in the woods and villages outside the city. This scene shows the aftermath of the skirmish as the paratroopers attempt to reinforce their positions for a possible renewed German onslaught. The most vivid memory for most American veterans of the Battle of the Bulge was the misery of life in the foxholes. It was commonplace for a unit to move every few days, and sometimes even more than once a day. Each move was accompanied by the need to dig another set of foxholes and defensive positions (2). While foxholes were useful in providing protection from German infantry attack, the main killer in the Ardennes fighting on both sides was artillery. Artillery was particularly deadly in wooded areas, since detonations in the trees tended to spray the area with wood splinters. Not only were these splinters deadly against unprotected infantry, but even if the infantryman was only wounded (3), the small splinters of wood were difficult for medics (4) to find and remove and so often led to life-threatening infections. The best protection against this scourge was the foxhole. The standard US Army practice was a two-man foxhole, deep enough to stand in. If a unit was stationary for any period of time, the practice was usually to create two sets of defenses – a deep fighting foxhole, and a long, shallow trench for sleeping, preferably with overhead cover such as logs. GIs were issued either the pre-war style of "T" handled entrenching shovel, or the later M1943 type (5) that had a folding blade. Neither was particularly effective, especially in frozen ground full of tree roots. The 101st Airborne Division was hastily deployed to the Ardennes after months of fighting in the Netherlands. By this stage, their distinctive paratrooper garb had given way to the same types of uniforms worn by other US infantry. This was especially true of new replacements and the glider infantry. One of the major scandals of the Ardennes was the poor preparation of the US Army in providing adequate winter clothing. A particular problem in the winter of 1944–45 was the inadequate supply of water-resistant winter boots. This led to high levels of trench foot in US infantry units. In the background are a pair of burning PzKpfw IV tanks (6). Although overshadowed by the larger Panther tank, the PzKpfw IV was still the workhorse of the Wehrmacht, and the most common German tank type in the Ardennes fighting. Hidden in the tree line is a M18 76mm gun motor carriage (7). This tank destroyer was the fastest tracked combat vehicle of World War II, designed to fulfill the Tank Destroyer Command's motto of "Seek, strike, destroy". In fact, by the time it entered service, its effectiveness was undermined by the inadequate performance of its gun against the new generation of German armored vehicles such as the Panther and the Jagdpanzer IV/70. The more powerful M36 tank destroyer with its 90mm gun was the preferred choice in the winter of 1944–45. (Peter Dennis)

paratroopers and infantry along the front line who would often see the Germans moving about in the open without any response. The situation became so bad that one regimental commander pleaded with McAuliffe for artillery support only to be told; "if you see 400 Germans in a 100-yard area and they have their heads up, you can fire artillery at them, but only two rounds!" McAuliffe's primary concern was that ammunition would run out before Patton's Third Army arrived.

After two days of skirmishing, significant German attacks resumed on 23 December. In the late afternoon, Kampfgruppe Hauser made another attempt to push into Marvie on the southern side of the city, supported by GR.39 to the west. German infantry attempted to stealthily probe past the scattered US outposts and once in position, a pair of assault guns came clanking up the road but were halted by a wrecked half-track that blocked the approach. A platoon from G/327th Glider Infantry was overwhelmed on Hill 500 after dark, and the attack penetrated into Marvie. Two M4 tanks from Team O'Hara discouraged any further advance into the village, but German attacks continued in earnest until midnight, and controlled the southern fringe of the village through the following day in spite of US efforts. Kampfgruppe Hauser had a hard time reinforcing the operation with any armor, as the area was heavily wooded with only a single road into the village.

On the night of 22/23 December, a "Russian High", a high-pressure front bringing cold weather and clearing skies, arrived and changed the fortunes of war. The next morning, a wave of 16 C-47 transports appeared over Bastogne, dropping the first batch of supplies. By dusk, 241 aircraft had flown to Bastogne dropping 441 tons of supplies. Drops the following day by 160 aircraft added 100 tons of supplies.

Kokott was convinced that any further assaults into the southern sector of Bastogne would be futile, so he proposed to Manteuffel that the next attack would be conducted where he suspected the Americans were

Paratroopers of the 101st Airborne Division recover supplies after the airdrop of 27 December along the Bastogne perimeter. (NARA)

The catastrophic effects of an ammunition fire and explosion are all too evident from the shattered hulk of this PzKpfw IV of Kampfgruppe Maucke, 15th Panzergrenadier Division knocked out north of Bastogne during the engagement with the 101st Airborne Division at Christmas Day.

weakest, in the northwest. He hoped that he would be able to use whatever armor was available, since the terrain in the northwest was much more favorable for tanks, and the cold weather was hardening the ground. In fact, the US defenses were probably best in this sector. Impressed by Kokott's determination, Manteuffel promised that the 15th Panzergrenadier Division would be put at his disposal for this attack. The 15th Panzergrenadier Division had recently arrived from the Italian Front, and was both experienced and well-equipped. The attack was scheduled for Christmas Day and Manteuffel grimly relayed Hitler's message that "Bastogne must be taken at all costs." The lead elements of the 15th Panzergrenadier Division arrived on the northern side of Bastogne shortly

Trench foot was a significant cause of US casualties in the Ardennes fighting that could be prevented by proper foot care. This corporal of the 327th Glider Infantry is drying his feet while serving along the Bastogne perimeter.

before midnight on Christmas Eve. The reinforcements included Kampfgruppe Maucke with two battalions of infantry, a tank battalion with about 30 tanks and tank destroyers, and two artillery battalions. Kokott decided to launch the attack in the pre-dawn hours since otherwise the armor would attract the attention of American fighter-bombers that were now swarming over the battlefield in the clear skies. With so little time to deploy, many of the troops of Panzergrenadier Regt.115 rode the Panzers into the attack zone.

McAuliffe received first news of the attack at 03.30hrs on Christmas Day, when A/502nd PIR in Rolle reported that the Germans were on top of them and then the line went dead. The regimental headquarters alerted the rest of the companies with orders to send reinforcements to Rolle. The battalion HQ hesitated to rush another company into the fight in the dark until it became clearer where the Germans were actually attacking and in what numbers. At dawn, this became clear when tanks of Kampfgruppe Maucke were spotted moving near the junction of the 502nd PIR and the 327th Glider Infantry. There were three principal thrusts, the 15th Panzergrenadier Division attack furthest west between Champs and Hemroulle, an initial GR.77 attack in the center coming down the road into Champs, and a smaller attack by GR.77 that began around 05.00 when Germany infantry infiltrated through some woods between Champs and Longchamps. The most serious threat came from the Panzer attack that rolled right over A/327th GIR. However, the Panzergrenadiers did not drive out the infantry, and when the next wave of Panzergrenadiers approached the Co. A positions on foot, they were greeted with intense rifle fire. The 15th Panzergrenadier Division tank attack split up, some tanks heading towards Hemroulle and others to rear of the B/502nd PIR. Two M18s from 705th Tank Destroyer Battalion knocked out a few of the advancing Panzers but were in turn knocked out when they tried to withdraw. Before reaching the woods where C/502nd PIR was deployed, the tanks veered northward towards Champs, exposing

Another PzKpfw IV named *Lustmolch* (Happy Salamander) of Kampfgruppe Maucke, 15th Panzergrenadier Division abandoned in Champs during the fighting with the 502nd IR on Christmas Day.

their flanks to rifle fire from the woods and to a pair of M18s from 705th Tank Destroyer Battalion. The Panzergrenadiers on the tanks took the worst beating from intense small arms fire, while three PzKpfw IVs were knocked out by gunfire and two more by bazookas at close range. A single PzKpfw IV broke into Champs but was stopped by 57mm anti-tank gunfire and bazookas.

The group of tanks and Panzergrenadiers that had split off earlier towards the 327th GIR received a far hotter reception. Four tank destroyers were located between Cos. A and B, and Co. C received support from a pair of M4 tanks that arrived shortly before the German attack. None of the German tanks survived the encounter, two being hit point-blank by 105mm howitzers, and the rest being knocked out by tank destroyers and bazookas. Not one of the 18 PzKpfw IV that started the attack survived, and most of the Panzergrenadiers were either killed or captured. The Christmas attack was the last major assault until Patton's relief column arrived.

The Air Campaign

The weather for the first week was too poor for the Luftwaffe to have any significant impact on the battle and only 170 sorties were conducted on the first day of the offensive. On 17 December, 600 daylight sorties were flown including some strafing missions, and these were followed after dark by over 250 ground-attack missions by night-fighters striking at major communication centers such as Liege. The plan was to keep at least 150 fighters in the air at all times during daylight to provide an aerial umbrella for the Panzer divisions, but this was seldom achieved and the number of sorties continued to decline. The US 9th Air Force also had its close-support operations hampered by the weather as well, and it was distracted by the unusually large numbers of German fighters active over the battlefield. Its two tactical air commands (TAC) flew about 450 tactical sorties daily for the first week of the offensive, mainly fighter sweeps with few ground-attack missions. When the weather finally cleared on 23 December, both the IX and XXIX TAC turned out in force including 669 fighter-bomber sorties. Medium bombers from IX Bomber Command conducted interdiction missions against German supply lines, but were met by furious resistance from German fighters, losing 35 bombers and suffering damage to 182 more out of the 624 that took part. As a result, on Christmas Eve, the 8th Air Force conducted 1,400 bomber sorties against 12 Luftwaffe airfields over the Rhine to dampen down Luftwaffe activity. Four of the airfields suffered little damage, but the other eight were shut down on average for eight days. On Christmas Day, American air activity reached levels not seen since the August missions against the Falaise gap, totaling 6,194 tactical sorties including 4,281 fighter sorties. Oberst Ludwig Heilmann of the 5th Fallschirmjäger Division grimly recalled that by nightfall, the attacking *Jabos* had left "an uninterrupted trail of burning vehicles extending like a torchlight procession from Bastogne all the way back to the Westwall … in my opinion, the Ardennes offensive was irretrievably lost when the Allies sent their air forces into action on 25 December, a fact that even the simplest soldier realized."

The Luftwaffe was powerless to stop this, as their inadequately trained fighter pilots suffered disproportionate losses in encounters with the more numerous US fighters. Allied fighters claimed to have shot down

On 19 December, the 353rd Fighter Squadron attempted to bomb the headquarters of the 116th Panzer Division but was bounced by about 40 Luftwaffe fighters. In the ensuing melee, the outnumbered but more experienced squadron downed nine German fighters while losing three Thunderbolts. This is *Big Jake*, the P-47D of Lt Lloyd Overfield, credited with two fighters that day, and seen here taxying at Rosieres during the Battle of the Bulge. (NARA)

718 German aircraft from 17 to 27 December, while losing 111 aircraft to German fighters and 307 more to other causes. A post-war RAF history of the Luftwaffe pungently noted that "bad servicing of the Luftwaffe's aircraft was becoming more widespread, and the pilots were all too ready to seize on the slightest excuse for returning early from their missions. Many pilots, insufficiently trained as they were, had no zest for facing the heavy Allied air onslaught which was carried out during the four days of good weather, December 24–27." A total of 346 fighter pilots were lost between 23 and 27 December, including 106 on Christmas Eve, the worst losses during a very costly month for the Luftwaffe fighter force. By the beginning of January, the Allied air forces had conducted about 34,100 missions including 16,600 tactical sorties over the Ardennes compared to 7,500 for the Luftwaffe. The Wehrmacht received little solace from the heightened Luftwaffe activity since so few of the missions were ground-attack.

The last great Luftwaffe operation in the west was conducted on New Year's Day when Jagdkorps 2 finally staged Operation Bodenplatte two weeks late. The attack included every serviceable fighter in the west, totaling about 1,035 aircraft including pathfinders. The attack caught the Allied air bases in Belgium and Holland napping, and 144 American and British aircraft were destroyed on the ground, 62 damaged, and a further 70 lost in aerial combat. But it was a Pyrrhic victory for the Luftwaffe. Over a third of the attack force was lost, some 304 aircraft, including 85 shot down by their own flak. A total of 214 aircrew were killed or captured, including three Geschwader commanders, all six Gruppe commanders, and 11 Staffel commanders – an irreplaceable loss. Bodenplatte had a crippling effect on subsequent Luftwaffe operations in the west; in contrast Allied losses were replaced quickly from depots and few aircrew had been lost.

OPERATION *BODENPLATTE*, NEW YEAR'S DAY 1945
(pages 62–63)

At 09.30hrs on New Year's Day, the Luftwaffe staged its long delayed attack on Allied airfields, codenamed *Bodenplatte* (baseplate). Among the participants were the Me-262A-2a fighter-bombers (1) of KG51, one of Hitler's new wonder weapons. Twenty-one of these aircraft took part in attacks on RAF airfields at Eindhoven and Heesch in the Netherlands. The Eindhoven strike was conducted in conjunction with Bf-109 and FW-190 fighters (2) of Jagdgeschwader 3 and was the more successful of the two missions, destroying or damaging about 50 of the Typhoons (3) and Spitfires stationed with the three wings there. The attack on Heesch with Jagdgeschwader 6 had little effect and one Me-262 was lost to ground fire. Kampfgeschwader 51 was the principal Luftwaffe unit operating the fighter-bomber version of the Me-262 at the time, and it was responsible for the majority of Me-262 sorties in late 1944. The I Gruppe flew from the Rheine and Hopsten airbases while II Gruppe flew from Hesepe. These fighter-bombers were used repeatedly in ground-attack missions in the Ardennes, though there is little evidence to suggest they were very effective in this role given the difficulty of delivering unguided bombs at high speed and at low altitude. KG 51 lost a total of five aircraft during the Ardennes missions in December: four to fighters and one to flak. The origins of the fighter-bomber version of the Me-262 were controversial. Although the aircraft had been designed from the outset as a fighter, Hitler was insistent that the aircraft be used as a fighter-bomber as well. This version could carry two 550lb bombs (4) under the nose and additional fuel to extend its range. However, two of its four 30mm cannon were deleted to save weight (5). It was far from ideal as a fighter-bomber, since the pilot had a difficult time aiming against the target except in low-altitude strikes or from a shallow dive. The first of these aircraft were deployed with Erprobungskommando Schenk (test detachment Schenk) in France in late July 1944, becoming redesignated as I/KG 51 in mid-August. The handful of aircraft were used in occasional ground-attack missions against Allied forces throughout August, and one of the new jet fighter-bombers was spotted and forced down by a US P-47 fighter on 28 August 1944 near Brussels. The Me-262A-2a seen here wears the distinctive markings of KG 51. The unit markings include the white tip on the nose and tail (6). The unit codes on the fuselage side (7) are the four-letter style, in this case 9K+CP with the 9K identifying KG 51, the third enlarged letter identifying the individual aircraft, and the final letter indicating the Staffel (H, K, L, M, N, P). The camouflage finish is typical of this period: RLM 76 light blue on the undersides, with RLM 81 brown-violet and 82 dark green on the upper surfaces and extending down the sides in an irregular spray-painted mottled pattern. (Howard Gerrard)

PATTON STRIKES BACK

The Third Army began moving its III Corps towards Arlon on 19 December. The spearhead of the northern attack was Patton's favorite, the 4th Armored Division. Muscle came from the 26th and 80th Divisions, reinforced by three field artillery groups. The attack was launched in the late afternoon of 21 December by all three divisions, with the corps advancing from three to five miles. The following day, the 4th Armored Division reached Martelange 13 miles south of Bastogne, the 26th Division moved up alongside it to the east and the 80th Division took Heiderscheid. As the III Corps approached Bastogne, German resistance intensified. By 23 December, elements from Brandenberger's 7th Army were finally approaching the southern outskirts of Bastogne, and the 5th Fallschirmjäger Division was assigned to cover the main road from Arlon through Marvie into Bastogne. Combat Command A took this route, but was halted by determined German resistance around Livarchamps. Recognizing that this route was the one most likely to be contested, the two other combat commands were sent up alternate routes. CCB went across country from Habay-la-Neuve but was stopped near Hompré. CCR was redeployed on Christmas, and after a 30-mile road march to the west, resumed its attack along the narrow Cobreville–Assenois road into southwestern Bastogne.

By the morning of 26 December, CCR was the closest of the three combat commands to Bastogne, and by mid-afternoon fought its way to within a short distance of the Bastogne defense. A task force was formed under Captain William Dwight consisting of Co. C, 37th Tank Battalion, and Co. C, 53rd AIB, which set off for Assenois at 16.10 after a preliminary artillery strike. The tanks proceeded into the village even before the artillery fire had lifted, avoiding much German resistance. Once the artillery lifted, the German defenders tried to disable the armored infantry column by throwing Teller mines underneath their half-tracks, blowing up one with mines, and knocking out three more with Panzerfaust anti-tank

Patton's initial assault against the 7th Army by the 80th Division led to a series of sharp battles along the Luxembourg border with the 352nd Volksgrenadier Division, supported on 23 December by Panzers of the Führer Grenadier Brigade. This StuG III assault gun is inspected by GIs of 2/319th Infantry in Heiderscheid a few days later. (NARA)

A Kampfgruppe of the Führer Grenadier Brigade attacked Patton's 80th Division in Heiderscheid on Christmas Eve and amongst its losses were the StuG III to the left and this SdKfz 251 half-track, one of the rare SdKfz 251/17 variants with a turreted 2cm autocannon. (NARA)

A group of prisoners from the 1/GR.914, 352nd Volksgrenadier Division, captured near Mertzig on 24 December by the 319th Infantry, 80th Division during Patton's drive to relieve Bastogne. (MHI)

rockets. But the American infantry drove out the defenders in bitter house-to-house fighting and 428 prisoners were taken. By late afternoon, Captain Dwight was greeted by the commander of the 101st Airborne, General McAuliffe in the outskirts of Bastogne. Shortly after midnight, the task force attacked the woods north of Assenois and by 03.00, the road was clear for vehicular traffic. The light tanks of Co. D/37th Tank Battalion escorted a relief column into Bastogne consisting of 40 supply trucks and 70 ambulances later in the day. While CCR had managed to break into Bastogne, it would take several more days of hard fighting to secure and widen the corridor. However, German forces in this sector were the weakest of the siege force, and the corridor was never seriously threatened. While this was not the end to the fighting for Bastogne, clearly the momentum was shifting in favor of the US Army.

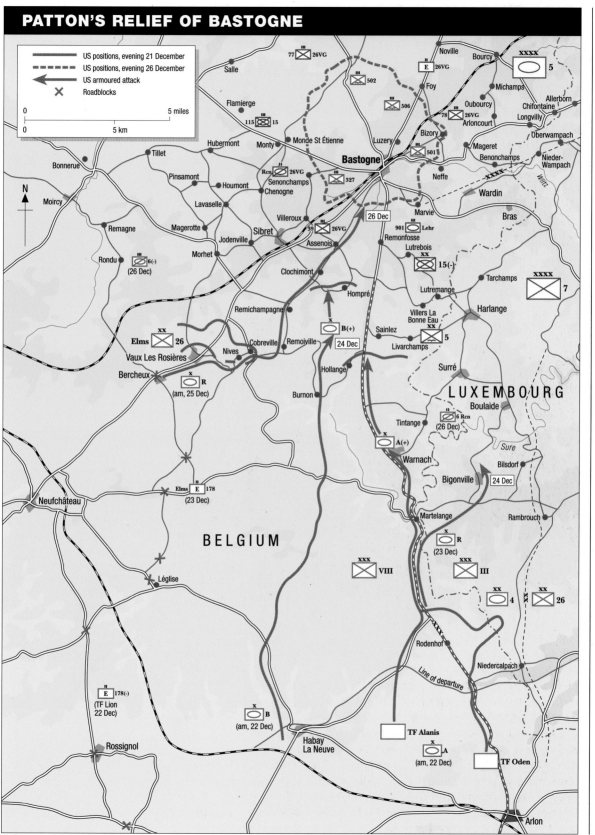

US positions, evening 21 December
US positions, evening 26 December
US armoured attack
Roadblocks

0 _____ 5 miles
0 _____ 5 km

N

Salle
77 26VG
Noville
Bourcy
E 26VG
Foy
502
Flamierge
506
Michamps
Allerborn
Chifontaine
Longvilly
Oubourcy
78 26VG
Arloncourt
Oberwampach
115 15
Monte St Étienne
Luzery
Bizory
Mageret
Nieder-Wampach
Benonchamps
Hubermont
Monty
501
Tillet
Bonnerue
Moircy
Houmont
Rcn 26VG
Senonchamps
Bastogne
Neffe
Wardin
Chenogne
327
Marvie
Bras
Pinsamont
Lavaselle
Villeroux
26 Dec
901 Lehr
Remonfosse
Magerotte
Jodenville
39 26VG
Assenois
Lutrebois
Tarchamps
Remagne
Sibret
15(-)
Rondu
6(-)
(26 Dec)
Morhet
Clochimont
Lutremange
7
Hompré
Lutremange
Remichampagne
Villers La
Bonne Eau
Harlange
26 Dec
Elms 26
Cobreville
Remoiville
x B(+)
24 Dec
Sainlez
5
Livarchamps
Vaux Les Rosières
Nives
Surré
Bercheux
x R
(am, 25 Dec)
Hollange
LUXEMBOURG
Burnon
Boulaide
Tintange
6 Rcn
(26 Dec)
Sure
x A(+)
Warnach
Bilsdorf
Neufchâteau
Elms E 178
(23 Dec)
Bigonville
24 Dec
Martelange
Rambrouch
BELGIUM
x R
(23 Dec)
XXX VIII
XXX III
Léglise
xx 4
xx 26
Rodenhof
Niedercalpach
E 178(-)
(TF Lion
22 Dec)
Line of departure
x B
(am, 22 Dec)
Rossignol
Habay
La Neuve
TF Alanis
x A
(am, 22 Dec)
TF Oden
Arlon

The first US tank into Bastogne was this M4A3E2 assault tank named Cobra King of Lt Charles Boggess from Co. C, 37th Tank Battalion, 4th Armored Division. (Patton Museum)

A column of tanks from the 4th Armored Division move through Bastogne with an M4A3E2 assault tank, possibly Cobra King, in the lead. (MHI)

The Struggle for the Tailles Plateau

When the "Russian High" arrived on the night of 22/23 December, the rain-soaked, muddy fields began to harden. This improved the prospects for German mobile operations since the Panzer columns were no longer trapped on the roads, and no longer obliged to fight for every village and road junction. While the cold weather restored some fluidity to the battle, it also led to clearing conditions that permitted Allied fighter-bombers to return to the fray, with frightful consequences for exposed German supply columns in the Eifel. The change in the weather had an immediate and dramatic impact on the fighting in the central sector of the Ardennes front, the battle for road junctions along the eastern edge of the Tailles plateau stretching towards Marche. This road net roughly paralleled the front line running from Trois Ponts in the north, west through Bra, Manhay, Grandmenil, Erezée, Hotton, and finally to

Marche. These road junctions were a German tactical objective since they controlled access to routes leading north and west towards the Meuse.

Krüger's 58th Panzer Corps made the initial breakthrough in this sector, with the 116th Panzer Division pushing past Houfallize on 19 December and reaching Hotton on 21 December with the 560th VG Div. to its right. Hotton was weakly defended by headquarters elements of the 3rd Armored Division, but the advance guard of the 116th Panzer Division was not strong enough to capture the town. Likewise, task forces of the 3rd Armored Division at Soy and Amonines stopped the 560th Volksgrenadier Division. Although Model had hoped to commit the II SS-Panzer Corps into this sector to reinforce this breakthrough since 20 December, lack of fuel and the continued hold-out of US forces in the St Vith salient blocked access from the northern sector of the Ardennes

RIGHT **One of the classic images from the Battle of the Bulge as two armored doughs from the 10th Armored Infantry Battalion, 4th Armored Division take aim at targets in the field outside Bastogne on 27 December 1944. (NARA)**

BELOW **A company of the 10th Armored Infantry Battalion, 4th Armored Division approaches Bastogne on 27 December and an explosion can be seen in the distance. (NARA)**

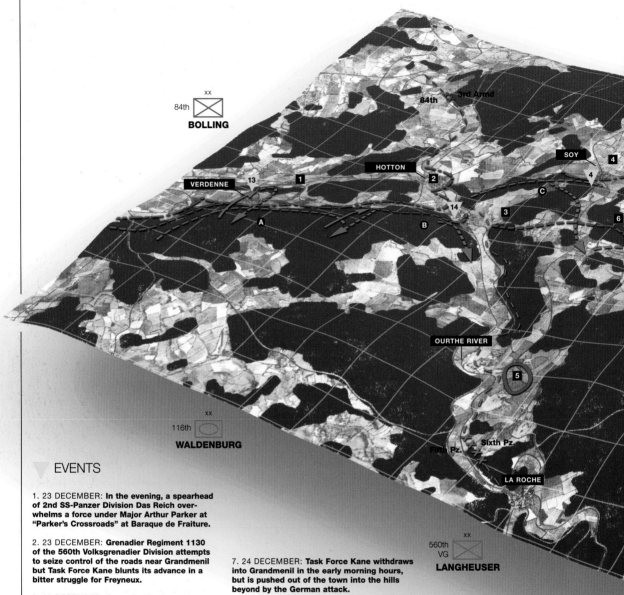

84th **3rd Armd**

84th BOLLING

SOY

HOTTON

VERDENNE

OURTHE RIVER

116th WALDENBURG

Fifth Pz. Sixth Pz.

LA ROCHE

560th VG LANGHEUSER

▼ EVENTS

1. 23 DECEMBER: **In the evening, a spearhead of 2nd SS-Panzer Division Das Reich overwhelms a force under Major Arthur Parker at "Parker's Crossroads" at Baraque de Fraiture.**

2. 23 DECEMBER: **Grenadier Regiment 1130 of the 560th Volksgrenadier Division attempts to seize control of the roads near Grandmenil but Task Force Kane blunts its advance in a bitter struggle for Freyneux.**

3. 23 DECEMBER: **Grenadier Regiment 1128 of the 560th Volksgrenadier Division attempts to take Amonines, but is beaten back by Task Force Orr of CCB, 3rd Armored Division.**

4. 23 DECEMBER: **Grenadier Regiment 1129 of the 560th Volksgrenadier Division attempts to take Soy, but is forced to retreat by elements of the CCR, 3rd Armored Division. These attacks continue through Christmas.**

5. **Elements from the 7th Armored Division, including a C/40th Tank Battalion are overwhelmed in the dark by the spearhead of the 2nd SS-Panzer Division Das Reich moving on Manhay, losing 21 of their 32 tanks.**

6. NIGHT, 23 DECEMBER: **Before they can conduct their planned withdrawal, Task Force Brewster is already outflanked by an attack of a Kampfgruppe of SS-Panzergrenadier Regiment 3, 2nd SS-Panzer Division. The troops abandon their vehicles and escape on foot.**

7. 24 DECEMBER: **Task Force Kane withdraws into Grandmenil in the early morning hours, but is pushed out of the town into the hills beyond by the German attack.**

8. 24 DECEMBER: **2nd SS-Panzer Division Das Reich fights its way into Manhay but fails to gain access to the Liege road beyond.**

9. 25 DECEMBER: **The battle turns to a stalemate on Christmas day when attacks by the 289th Infantry and Task Force McGeorge against Grandmenil and CCA, 7th Armored Division fail, as do efforts by the 2nd SS-Panzer Division to break out of the town towards the west.**

10. 26 DECEMBER: **An attack by SS-Panzergrenadier Regiment 4 against the 325th Glider Infantry in Tri-le-Cheslaing fails.**

11. 26 DECEMBER: **Task Force McGeorge and Panzers of the 2nd SS-Panzer Division clash again in the first skirmish of the day, but renewed American attacks later in the day in conjunction with the 3/289th Infantry puts the US partly in control of Grandmenil by dusk.**

12. 26 DECEMBER: **The 3/517th Parachute Infantry, 82nd Airborne Division, finally regains Manhay after nightfall.**

13. 26 DECEMBER: **After its Kampfgruppe Bayer is trapped north of Verdenne in a failed attack on 24 December, the badly weakened 116th Panzer Division tries to relieve them, but is beaten back again by the 334th Infantry. Kampfgruppe Bayer is given permission to escape after dark.**

14. **The Fuhrer Begleit Brigade joins the attack on the road junctions trying to seize Hotton, but is stopped. At dusk, it is ordered to back up and head for Bastogne to join the siege there.**

BATTLE FOR THE ROAD JUNCTIONS

23–27 December 1944, viewed from the southeast. When US forces withdraw from the St Vith salient on 23 December, they permit the injection of the II SS-Panzer Corps into the battle for the key road junctions on the Tailles plateau. In a series of bitter skirmishes around Christmas, the Waffen-SS Panzer units fight their way into several of the key towns while neighboring units of the 5th Panzer Army do likewise further west. But in the days after Christmas, US counter-attacks push them back out of these towns.

Note gridlines are shown at intervals of 1 mile/1.61km

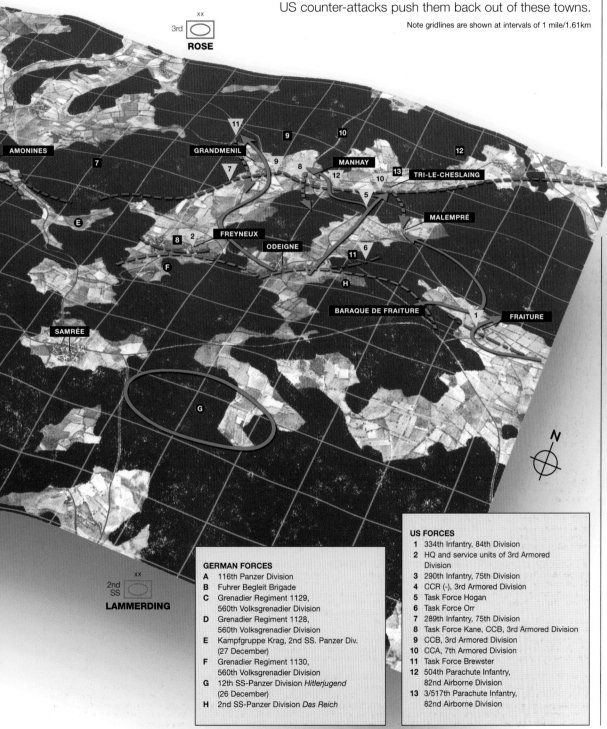

GERMAN FORCES

A   116th Panzer Division
B   Fuhrer Begleit Brigade
C   Grenadier Regiment 1129,
    560th Volksgrenadier Division
D   Grenadier Regiment 1128,
    560th Volksgrenadier Division
E   Kampfgruppe Krag, 2nd SS. Panzer Div.
    (27 December)
F   Grenadier Regiment 1130,
    560th Volksgrenadier Division
G   12th SS-Panzer Division *Hitlerjugend*
    (26 December)
H   2nd SS-Panzer Division *Das Reich*

US FORCES

1   334th Infantry, 84th Division
2   HQ and service units of 3rd Armored
    Division
3   290th Infantry, 75th Division
4   CCR (-), 3rd Armored Division
5   Task Force Hogan
6   Task Force Orr
7   289th Infantry, 75th Division
8   Task Force Kane, CCB, 3rd Armored Division
9   CCB, 3rd Armored Division
10 CCA, 7th Armored Division
11 Task Force Brewster
12 504th Parachute Infantry,
    82nd Airborne Division
13 3/517th Parachute Infantry,
    82nd Airborne Division

into the central area between the Salm and Meuse rivers. From the Allied perspective, the salient had been held far longer than expected, and with the defenses on the verge of collapse, Montgomery authorized a withdrawal.

When the ground froze on the night of 22/23 December, the trapped CCB, 7th Armored Division, and the other units in the St Vith salient could finally pull back over the Salm. With the obstruction posed by the St Vith salient removed, Obergruppenführer Bittrich's 2nd SS-Panzer Corps began to flood into the vacuum created by the US withdrawal into the area from the Salm to the Ourthe river. The objective of the II SS-Panzer Corps was to further rupture the US defensive lines in the La Gleize–Bra–Erezée–Marche area with a secondary, if somewhat hopeless, mission of relieving Kampfgruppe Peiper trapped in La Gleize. With the prospects for the I SS-Panzer Corps growing increasingly poor, it was becoming clear to Berlin that the failure of Dietrich's 6th Panzer Army was having a ripple effect by exposing the advances of Manteuffel's 5th Panzer Army, since their lines of communication were now vulnerable to US reinforcements pouring in from the north. Model and Rundstedt wanted the II SS-Panzer Corps to gain control of the road net on the Tailles plateau to weaken US armored attacks against the 5th Panzer Army from the north.

The 2nd SS-Panzer Division *Das Reich* began moving over the Salm River on 23 December heading for the Baraque de Fraiture crossroads, while the neighboring 9th SS-Panzer Division *Hohenstaufen* moved to its right, against the withdrawing St Vith garrison and the 82nd Airborne Division. The roadblock at Baraque de Fraiture was held by a small detachment from the 589th Field Artillery led by Major Arthur Parker, and reinforced by some tanks from TF Kane of the 3rd Armored Division. The crossroads was at a key junction between the 3rd Armored Division and 82nd Airborne Division, but was weakly held due to a lack of resources. On the afternoon of 23 December, "Parker's Crossroads" was pummeled by German artillery for 20 minutes and then assaulted by a Panzergrenadier regiment supported by two tank companies. As this

position was overwhelmed after nightfall, it opened the door to Manhay, which controlled access to the road leading to Liege.

The 560th VG Div., the easternmost element of the 5th Panzer Army began the push against Manhay from the western side, attempting to seize villages on the approaches to the town. GR.1160 attempted a two-pronged attack on Freyneux, held by Task Force Kane of CCB, 3rd Armored Division. Although supported by assault guns, the attacks were beaten back by tank fire and the regiment suffered such heavy casualties that it was no longer effective. Further west, GR.1129 advanced towards Soy and Hotton, but the attack was held up by other elements of the 3rd Armored Division.

The American defenses around Manhay were in a confused state with elements of the XVIII Airborne Corps, including the 7th Armored Division withdrawing from the St Vith salient, intermingled with newly arrived and scattered task forces of the 3rd Armored Division under Collins' VII Corps. Field Marshal Montgomery was very unhappy about the weak and exposed defensive positions of the 82nd Airborne Division and on the morning of 24 December, he instructed Ridgway's XVIII Airborne Corps to pull back the scattered paratrooper detachments to a more defensible perimeter along the road from Trois Ponts to Manhay that night. Likewise, the 3rd Armored Division reorganized its defenses, reassigning elements of the 7th Armored Division to the defense of Manhay. Amidst this confusion, the 2nd SS-Panzer Division began its attack up the Manhay road.

SS-Oberführer Heinz Lammerding of *Das Reich* delayed the attack towards Manhay until a key bridge at Odeigne could be completed. With the new bridge in place, he waited until nightfall to begin the attack to avoid being pummeled by American *Jabos*. Christmas Eve in this sector was a clear, moonlit night with the ground frozen hard and covered by a thin layer of snow, in other words excellent for tank movement and well suited to night operations. SS-Panzergrenadier Regiment 3 *Deutschland* began moving up the road from Odeigne around 21.00hrs towards a roadblock of CCA, 7th Armored Division, which was in the process of pulling back as part of the reorganization. One of the German columns was led by a captured Sherman tank, and in the dark, the American tanks

thought the column was simply an American unit withdrawing as part of
the shuffle. The Germans began firing flares, and quickly decimated the
surprised American tanks at close range, overrunning the roadblock in
the process. There was poor coordination between the 3rd Armored
Division and CCA, 7th Armored Division, about the withdrawal around
Manhay, and in the pre-dawn hours SS-Panzergrenadier Regiment 3 was
able to exploit the confusion and push into Manhay itself.

TF Brewster, the most exposed of the US outposts, began to withdraw
not realizing that the area between them and the rest of the 3rd Armored
Div. had been flooded by advancing German troops. When the two lead
tanks were knocked out and blocked the retreat route, Brewster ordered
his troops to abandon their vehicles and infiltrate back to US lines as best
they could. Task Force Kane pulled back more successfully, but were
forced to give up Grandmenil due to the shortage of infantry. Fortunately,
infantry reinforcements from 289th Infantry, 75th Division, arrived shortly
afterwards and blocked the roads leading out of Grandmenil. When 2nd
SS-Panzer Division *Das Reich* attempted to push out the west side of town,
again using a captured Sherman tank in the lead, they were halted when
a lone bazookaman knocked out the lead tank. The road was constricted
on either side by steep slopes, so *Das Reich*'s column was effectively stopped
for the moment.

Although the *Das Reich* assault had managed to thoroughly disrupt the
planned American reorganization around Manhay, it fell far short of its
objectives of gaining the road exits out of Manhay and neighboring
Grandmenil northward, which were still firmly in American hands. On
Christmas Day, Obergruppenführer Bittrich received new orders. Instead
of pushing up the road to Liege, he was to turn his corps westward, down
along the road towards Erezée and Hotton, to strike the flank of Collins'
VII Corps, which at the time was closing in on the spearhead of
Manteuffel's 5th Panzer Army near the Meuse River. *Das Reich* spent
most of Christmas Day attempting to gain room to maneuver in the

A patrol by the 23rd Engineer Battalion on 7 January near the scene of the earlier fighting for "Parker's Crossroads" at Baraque de Fraiture. (MHI)

An armored dough of the 36th Armored Infantry, 3rd Armored Division mans a M1919A4 .30 cal Browning light machine-gun near Amonines while behind him is one of the division's M4 medium tanks.

Manhay–Grandmenil area prior to their new drive west, while the US forces attempted to reestablish a cohesive defense and push *Das Reich* out of Manhay and Grandmenil. An attempt to retake Grandmenil on Christmas afternoon by the 289th Infantry backed by tanks from TF McGeorge faltered when US aircraft accidentally bombed the US tanks. An attack into Manhay by CCA, 7th Armored Division, was stopped in the late afternoon after the lead tanks encountered road obstructions and were knocked out by German anti-tank guns. *Das Reich* had no more success in its efforts, as the hills overlooking the towns were peppered with US artillery observers who called in repeated howitzer strikes every time the Panzers attempted to move. When the artillery let up, the towns were hit by repeated US airstrikes, and Manhay and Grandmenil were turning into a killing ground. Plans to move the other main element of the corps, the 9th SS-Panzer Division *Hohenstaufen*, to the Manhay area to reinforce the planned drive on Erezée also failed. The fighting for the crossroads was turning into a bloody stalemate, but one that favored the Americans since they could move in more reinforcements. By Christmas, the US Army had 17 field artillery battalions in the area from the Aisne to the Lienne rivers, and much of this was within range of the stalled *Das Reich*.

To the west, the battered 560th VG Div. continued its attempts to win control of the road west of Erezée around Soy and Hotton from overextended elements of the 3rd Armored Division. TF Orr reported that on Christmas Eve, the German infantry had made 12 separate attacks to break through their defenses and that "if they'd have had three more riflemen, they'd probably have overrun our positions." The American defenses along the key road gradually began to solidify as the green 75th Division came into the line. Although the inexperienced troops took heavy casualties during their hasty introduction into combat, the added rifle strength considerably bolstered the American lines.

By 26 December, *Das Reich* could not wait any longer for the arrival of the 9th SS-Panzer Division, and early that morning deployed SS-Panzergrenadier Regiment 4 *Der Führer* against the 325th GIR to the east at Tri-le-Cheslaing. This attack was stopped cold. The main attack was a two-pronged effort emanating out of Grandmenil, one group straight down the main road towards Erezée and the other up a narrow

The fields around Amonines are littered with the wrecks of SdKfz 250 half-tracks of the 116th Panzer Division, destroyed during an encounter with Task Force Orr of the 3rd Armored Division. The vehicle to the left is an unusual variant with a 2cm cannon.

path towards Mormont intended to outflank the American defenses if the first attack did not succeed. The German attack out of Grandmenil coincided with an effort by TF McGeorge to retake the town, and a head-on tank duel ensued. The M4 tanks of TF McGeorge stood little chance in a direct confrontation with the *Das Reich* Panthers, and lost all but two M4 tanks in the brief encounter. However, the tank duel derailed the main German attack. The northern probe towards Mormont was stopped when a German tank was knocked out in a narrow gorge, blocking any further advance. Grandmenil was subjected to a barrage by three artillery battalions, and then assaulted again by 16 M4 tanks of TF McGeorge and 3/289th Infantry. The US infantry captured about half of Grandmenil and the access to the road to Manhay. The 7th Armored Division made a half-hearted attempt to reach the Grandmenil–Manhay road at the same time, but the badly battered unit could not put enough strength into the field, and the attack was halted by German tank fire. After Manhay was softened up with fighter-bomber strikes, the village was attacked by 3/517th PIR in the evening, and by dawn the paratroopers had pushed *Das Reich* out. By this stage, Bittrich realized that any effort to force open the road through Grandmenil was futile, and on the morning of 27 December, *Das Reich* was withdrawn. Furthermore, the operational objective of the attack, to relieve pressure on the 5th Panzer Army spearhead near the Meuse, had become pointless after the 2nd Panzer Division had been trapped and crushed in the days after Christmas by the US 2nd Armored Division. Further attacks were attempted, including an assault on Sadzot on 28 December, but the II SS-Panzer Corps had reached its high-water mark days before, and in early January Berlin began stripping SS-Panzer units out of the Ardennes to reinforce the threatened Russian front.

THE HIGH-WATER MARK

Late on the evening of 23 December, the reconnaissance battalion of the 2nd Panzer Division reported that it had approached to within nine kilometers of the Meuse River near Dinant. This would prove to be the high-water mark of the Ardennes offensive. The reconnaissance battalion of 2nd Panzer Division had reached and crossed the Ourthe River at Ourtheville on 21 December, followed by Panzergrenadiers later in the day. The advance beyond was slowed for more than a day by a lack of fuel. By 23 December, the division was again on the march in two columns, the main one along Route N4 to Marche and a smaller column to Hargimont. Present with the division was the impatient corps commander, General Lüttwitz, who relieved one of the regimental commanders when the pace of the advance was slowed by a weak American roadblock. While Hargimont was captured, Marche was stoutly defended by arriving elements of the 84th Division. Lüttwitz ordered Lauchert to turn the bulk of his division west towards Dinant and the Meuse, and to leave only a blocking force towards Marche. He hoped to deploy the 9th Panzer Division near Marche once it arrived. The division was preceded by Kampfgruppe Böhm consisting of its reconnaissance battalion reinforced with a few Panzers. On the night of 23/24 December, KG Böhm raced up the highway towards Dinant, finally reaching the woods near Foy-Notre Dame. It was followed on 24 December by the advance guard of the division, KG Cochenhausen, consisting of Panzergrenadier Regiment 304 and 1/Panzer Regiment 3.

Radio reports of the advance caused jubilation in Berlin. Hitler personally congratulated Rundstedt and Model, and freed up the 9th Panzer and 15th Panzergrenadier Divisions to reinforce the 5th Panzer Army. Model was under few illusions about reaching the "Grand Slam" or "Little Slam" objectives, but Panzers reaching the Meuse was enough of an accomplishment that it would help the Wehrmacht save face from all the disappointments of the campaign. Model immediately directed the 9th Panzer Division to follow the 2nd Panzer Division and protect its right flank from advancing American forces. As noted earlier, he ordered the entire 15th Panzergrenadier Division into the area north of Bastogne to finally crush the resistance there.

An M4A1 (76mm) of Task Force B, CCA, 2nd Armored Division carries infantry into an assault near Frandeux on 27 December during the attempts to contain the Panzer Lehr Division near Rochefort. (NARA)

SPEARHEAD TO THE MEUSE (pages 78–79)

Kampfgruppe Böhm races to the Meuse in the days before Christmas 1944. This battlegroup was based around the 2nd Panzer Division's reconnaissance battalion, Panzer Aufklärungs Abteilung 2, but its combat power was reinforced by a few Panther tanks from the division's Panzer regiment, Pz.Rgt.3. This was necessary as its reconnaissance battalion had been only partially refitted prior to the Ardennes operation. Its first company was absent and still refitting, while its third company was equipped mainly with bicycles. Ill-equipped or not, one of the reasons for the success of 5th Panzer Army in penetrating deep behind American lines was the more effective use of their reconnaissance units. Model's Army Group B headquarters was critical of poor use of reconnaissance units by the neighboring Waffen-SS Panzer divisions, which usually employed them like any other Panzer or Panzergrenadier formation. The regular army Panzer divisions had learned from hard experience that the primary job of the reconnaissance elements was to move fast and avoid unnecessary combat in order to fulfill their mission. The armored patrol seen here is led by a SdKfz 234 Puma armored car (1). This was one of most effective scout vehicles of World War II, armed with a 50mm gun (2).

Each of its eight wheels was independently sprung, and it had excellent mobility for a wheeled vehicle in terrain, and high travel speeds of over 50 mph when on roads. In the Ardennes, the division had ten of these armored cars as well as two of the related SdKfz 234/1 armed with a 20mm cannon, and two SdKfz 233 armed with a 75mm short gun. Following behind the Puma is a Panther Ausf. G tank (3). The 2nd Panzer Division started the offensive with 51 Panthers and 29 PzKpfw IV tanks. Behind the Panther is the lead SdKfz 251 armored half-track (4). Although more commonly associated with the Panzergrenadier regiment, this jack-of-all-trades was also used by scout units and there were 13 of these on hand at the beginning of the offensive. The more common armored half-track in the reconnaissance battalion was the SdKfz 250 light half-track with 33 in service in December 1944. The vehicles seen here mostly lack any distinctive tactical unit insignia since the division was re-equipped so soon before the start of the offensive. The Panther and Puma lack the usual tactical numbers on the turret, and the division's distinctive trident emblem is nowhere to be seen. The use of foliage for camouflage was common in the Ardennes, especially after 23 December when the clear weather marked the return of the dreaded American *Jabos*. (Peter Dennis)

A pair of GIs from the 207th Engineer Combat Battalion prepare a bazooka by fitting a battery into the launcher during the fighting near Buissonville on 29 December. (NARA)

But by this late date, the advance of the 2nd Panzer Division no longer had any strategic significance. There was no operational value in reaching the Meuse at Dinant, as the town was backed by high cliffs and could be easily defended by the Allies. Namur was even less attractive and its fortifications posed a substantial hurdle for any attacker. The spearhead Panzer divisions were exhausted, short of functional tanks and dangerously short of fuel. This was not immediately apparent to Hitler or the Allied commanders.

The threat of German units crossing the Meuse prompted Field Marshal Montgomery to begin redeploying his reserve, the British XXX Corps, on 19 December to cover the exits over the river. This took time, but by 23 December, the major river crossings at Givet, Dinant and Namur were each covered by tank battalions from the 29th Armoured Brigade, each reinforced by a rifle company.

By the time that KG Cochenhausen approached the Meuse, Allied reinforcements were becoming a growing threat. Its attack was constantly diluted by the need to detach units to fight off flank attacks by American units appearing in the area. One of its Panzer columns was wiped out in the pre-dawn hours when it stumbled into an advancing column from CCA, 2nd Armored Division, along the Ciney–Rochefort road. To make matters worse, the division was threatened from the rear when the 335th Infantry of the 84th Division began an attack near Marche that at one point captured the main supply road. Although elements of the 2nd Panzer Division managed to hold the road open, American pressure was increasing as more reinforcements arrived.

On the night of 23/24 December, a single captured jeep with a scout party of three German soldiers approached the bridge at Dinant, but were blown up when they ran over a mine planted by the British defenders. The advance of KG Böhm was finally brought to an end on the morning of 24 December. As one of its columns began probing towards the river crossing, their lead PzKpfw IV tank was destroyed by a Sherman 17-pdr of the British 3rd Royal Tank Regiment that had taken up defensive positions on the east bank of the river the day before. Later in the morning, two more Panthers were knocked out, and the 3 RTR roadblocks established the farthest advance point of the Wehrmacht during the Ardennes offensive. CCA, 2nd Armored Division, advanced down the Ciney–Rochefort road for most of Christmas Eve, joined up with the British tankers, and pushed on to Buissonville in the afternoon, threatening to isolate KG Cochenhausen.

By late on Christmas Eve, it had become clear to Lüttwitz that the advance had come to an end. By now he recognized that he was facing major opposition in the 2nd Armored Division and 84th Division. Instead of ordering the long-delayed Panzer Lehr Division to Celles to join with the 2nd Panzer Division to race for the Meuse, Lüttwitz realized he would need to block any further advance of the Americans to buy time for the vulnerable 2nd Panzer Division to return to the corps bridgehead at Rochefort. He hoped to take Humain and Buissonville,

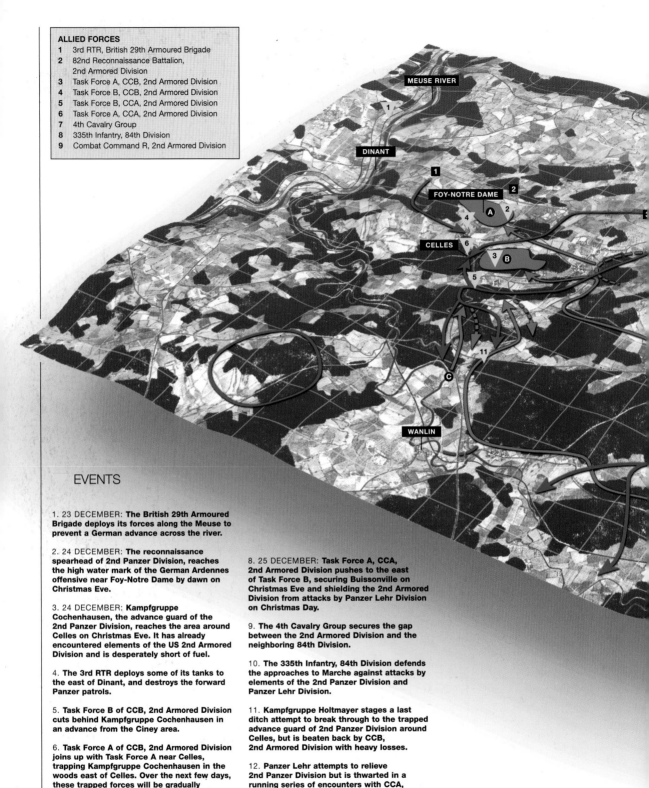

ALLIED FORCES

1 3rd RTR, British 29th Armoured Brigade
2 82nd Reconnaissance Battalion,
   2nd Armored Division
3 Task Force A, CCB, 2nd Armored Division
4 Task Force B, CCB, 2nd Armored Division
5 Task Force B, CCA, 2nd Armored Division
6 Task Force A, CCA, 2nd Armored Division
7 4th Cavalry Group
8 335th Infantry, 84th Division
9 Combat Command R, 2nd Armored Division

EVENTS

1. 23 DECEMBER: **The British 29th Armoured Brigade deploys its forces along the Meuse to prevent a German advance across the river.**

2. 24 DECEMBER: **The reconnaissance spearhead of 2nd Panzer Division, reaches the high water mark of the German Ardennes offensive near Foy-Notre Dame by dawn on Christmas Eve.**

3. 24 DECEMBER: **Kampfgruppe Cochenhausen, the advance guard of the 2nd Panzer Division, reaches the area around Celles on Christmas Eve. It has already encountered elements of the US 2nd Armored Division and is desperately short of fuel.**

4. **The 3rd RTR deploys some of its tanks to the east of Dinant, and destroys the forward Panzer patrols.**

5. **Task Force B of CCB, 2nd Armored Division cuts behind Kampfgruppe Cochenhausen in an advance from the Ciney area.**

6. **Task Force A of CCB, 2nd Armored Division joins up with Task Force A near Celles, trapping Kampfgruppe Cochenhausen in the woods east of Celles. Over the next few days, these trapped forces will be gradually squeezed and the pocket overwhelmed.**

7. 25 DECEMBER: **Task Force B of CCA, 2nd Armored Division departs Leignon on the morning of Christmas Eve and by Christmas Day is poised to cut off the 2nd Panzer Division from their staging area in Rochefort.**

8. 25 DECEMBER: **Task Force A, CCA, 2nd Armored Division pushes to the east of Task Force B, securing Buissonville on Christmas Eve and shielding the 2nd Armored Division from attacks by Panzer Lehr Division on Christmas Day.**

9. **The 4th Cavalry Group secures the gap between the 2nd Armored Division and the neighboring 84th Division.**

10. **The 335th Infantry, 84th Division defends the approaches to Marche against attacks by elements of the 2nd Panzer Division and Panzer Lehr Division.**

11. **Kampfgruppe Holtmayer stages a last ditch attempt to break through to the trapped advance guard of 2nd Panzer Division around Celles, but is beaten back by CCB, 2nd Armored Division with heavy losses.**

12. **Panzer Lehr attempts to relieve 2nd Panzer Division but is thwarted in a running series of encounters with CCA, 2nd Armored Division.**

13. 26–27 DECEMBER: **The 9th Panzer Division is added to the fray west of Marche leading to major tank skirmishes around Humain with CCA and CCR of the 2nd Armored Division.**

BLUNTING THE SPEARHEAD

24–27 December 1944, viewed from the southeast. The German offensive in the Ardennes reaches its high water mark on Christmas Eve when the spearhead units of the 2nd Panzer Division come within sight of the Meuse River near Dinant. Out of fuel, they are trapped near Celles by the 2nd Armored Division, which proceeds to beat up successive attempts by the 47th Panzer Corps to relieve the doomed battle groups near the Meuse.

Note gridlines are shown at intervals of 1 mile/1.61km

2nd Armd · HARMON

CINEY

LEIGNON

HAID

HAVERSIN

9

6

5

7

2nd Armd

84th

BAILLONVILLE

8

BUISSONVILLE

9

2

13

10

MARCHE

8

2nd · LAUCHERT

E

7

ROCHEFORT

12

JEMELLE

HARGIMONT

F

D

Panzer Lehr · BAYERLEIN

GERMAN FORCES
A Kampfgruppe Böhm, 2nd Panzer Division
B Kampfgruppe Cochenhausen, 2nd Panzer Division
C Kampfgruppe Holtmayer, 2nd Panzer Division
D Panzer Lehr Division
E 9th Panzer Division
F HQ and other elements of 2nd Panzer Division

83

Lt Robert Boscawen, commander of 2 Troop, the Coldstream Guards sits in a Sherman (17-pdr) guarding one of the bridges over the Meuse at Namur on Christmas Day. British armored units were deployed along the Meuse River in the days before Christmas to prevent a possible German crossing. (NARA)

thereby relieving pressure on the beleaguered 2nd Panzer Division. The desperately needed and long-delayed 9th Panzer Division was still behind schedule and lost another day when fuel could not be provided.

General Ernest Harmon of the 2nd Armored Division was itching to attack KG Cochenhausen after it was spotted by aerial reconnaissance. US units had intercepted German radio messages that made it very clear that the German units were seriously short of fuel. The opportunity to crush the Wehrmacht spearhead was almost thrown away. Montgomery was still concerned that the Germans were planning to throw their weight through the center and continue the advance towards Liege. Hodges had visited Collins on 23 December and knew that he wanted to attack the 2nd Panzer Division spearhead with the 2nd Armored Division. Yet in the wake of the fighting around Manhay, precipitated by the confused withdrawal on 23 December, Montgomery talked to Hodges about withdrawing VII Corps back to the Andenne–Hotton–Manhay line, not pushing forward. Montgomery's preoccupation with "tidying-up" the northern sector of the front so alarmed Bradley that he sent a note to Hodges that warned that while he was "no longer in my command, I would view with serious misgivings the surrender of any more ground". The following day, Montgomery reiterated his intent for the VII Corps to go over to the defensive. Hodges and the First Army staff were not enthusiastic to rein in Collins. A senior staff officer was sent to VII Corps headquarters with Montgomery's instructions, but First Army consciously neglected to forbid an attack, anticipating that the aggressive Collins would use his discretion to destroy the German spearhead. As Hodges' staff hoped, Collins ordered an attack. This decision proved timely as it allowed the 2nd Armored Division to beat up the weakened Panzer divisions of Lüttwitz's corps piecemeal rather than having to confront them simultaneously.

The 2nd Armored Division's main thrust on Christmas Day was conducted by CCB against KG Böhm and KG Cochenhausen, while CCA and the 4th Cavalry Group blocked Panzer Lehr Division and the newly

This Panther Ausf. G from the Panzer Lehr Division was knocked out during the attacks on Buissonville in the days after Christmas in the fighting with the 2nd Armored Division on the approaches to the Meuse. (NARA)

arrived 9th Panzer Division further east. CCB launched an enveloping attack out from Ciney in two task forces joining at Celles in the mid-afternoon and clearing the town. This trapped two large concentrations of 2nd Panzer Division units in the woods north of the town. Panzer Lehr Division attempted to push CCA out of Buissonville with an early morning attack at 07.50, but was repulsed with the loss of eight tanks, an assault gun and numerous infantry. A Panzergrenadier attack 40 minutes later was also hit hard, putting an end to attacks that day. Another battalion from Panzer Lehr was more successful at Humain, pushing a troop from the 4th Cavalry Group out of the village early on Christmas Day, and holding it against further attacks.

Lauchert formed KG Holtmayer from remaining elements of 2nd Panzer Division near Marche in hope of relieving the Celles pocket, and it departed Rochefort on the night of 25/26 December. It reached to within a kilometer of the Celles pocket but, without significant armored support, it was shattered by artillery and then roughly brushed off by CCB, 2nd Armored Division. To further seal off the pocket, on 27 December elements of the 4th Cavalry Group established a blocking position near Ciergnon and CCA, 2nd Armored Division, pushed south from Buissonville, reaching the 2nd Panzer Division's main assembly area in Rochefort. CCB, 2nd Armored Division, spent 26/27 December reducing the Celles pocket. At 15.30hrs on 26 December, the 2nd Panzer Division headquarters radioed survivors in the pocket to destroy any remaining heavy equipment and attempt to fight their way out. The trapped German units made two major break-out attempts on 26 December, but on 27 December the pocket began to collapse and about 150 tanks and vehicles were found destroyed or abandoned and 448 prisoners were taken. About 600 soldiers escaped from the woods on the nights of 26 and 27 December. By the end of December, the 2nd Panzer Division had been reduced in strength from about 120 tanks and assault guns to only about 20 and was no longer combat effective.

Panzer Lehr Division, reinforced by elements of the 9th Panzer Division, continued attempts to hold back the VII Corps attack. Harmon committed both CCA and CCR against Humain on 27 December, finally retaking the town from the 9th Panzer Division shortly before midnight. The neighboring 335th Infantry pushed down out of Marche, further sealing off the main highway onto the Marche plateau. Manteuffel by now realized that any further attempts to reach the Meuse would be futile, and his two best Panzer divisions were too weak for further offensive operations, with only about 50 operational Panzers.

SECURING BASTOGNE

The corridor between Patton's Third Army and Bastogne was precarious for the first few days, and was initially located on poor secondary roads. The last week of December was spent trying to gain control of the main roads, while at the same time both Manteuffel's 5th Panzer Army and Brandenberger's 7th Army desperately tried to sever the corridor. Manteuffel still held out hope that the "Little Slam" objectives might be reached, first by eliminating American resistance in Bastogne, then swinging back northwest toward Dinant. Model and Rundstedt agreed, adding a new 39th Panzer Corps headquarters under Generalleutnant Karl Decker to manage the units scraped together from elsewhere in the Ardennes. The Führer Begleit Brigade was assigned to the attack south of Bastogne, and other units moving into the area, included the badly decimated 1st SS-Panzer Division *Leibstandarte SS Adolf Hitler*, the 3rd Panzer Grenadier Division and the Führer Grenadier Brigade. The first attempt by Remer's Führer Begleit Brigade (FBB) was aborted after the unit was pounded by American fighter-bombers. On the US side, the CCA, 9th Armored Division, began a push out of Bastogne on the morning of 27 December to clear the western side of Bastogne, and spent three days grinding into the German defenses.

There were several strategic options for eliminating the "Bulge" in the Ardennes. Patton proposed the most ambitious, an attack by his Third Army from the area of Luxembourg City with a corresponding First Army lunge from the northern shoulder, joining at St Vith and entrapping as much of the 5th and 6th Panzer Armies as possible. This

GIs from the 84th Division dig in after a skirmish along a tree line near Berismenil on 13 January that left the GI in the foreground dead. The division advanced as far as Grande Morment the next day, before halting to recuperate after weeks of hard fighting in the Ardennes.

A patrol from the 101st Airborne Division moves out of Bastogne during the fighting on 29 December. (NARA)

A .30cal. machine-gun team of the 3/289th Infantry, 75th Division has set up in a house in Salmchateau on 16 January during the fighting to link up with Patton's Third Army. (NARA)

operation was never seriously entertained by Bradley or Eisenhower as there were serious doubts that such a mobile operation could be supported in the winter months over the restricted road network in Luxembourg and in the Elsenborn Ridge/Hohes Venn area as well as the recognition that the Germans could withdraw faster than the US Army could advance. Both Collins and Ridgway were anxious to start offensive operations after Christmas, but Montgomery remained fearful that the Germans might still break through somewhere along the First Army's extended defensive perimeter. The First Army Corps commanders doubted the Germans had the resources and held a more realistic appreciation of the solidity of the First Army defenses. When pressed by Collins about a possible attack from the Tailles Plateau towards St Vith to cut off the German offensive at its base, Montgomery said: "Joe, you can't supply a corps along a single road" to which Collins "in disrespectful exasperation" replied "well Monty, maybe you British can't, but we can." Patience with Montgomery's stalling of offensive operations by the First Army made Eisenhower rue the day he had turned over command of the First Army to him. Collins offered Hodges three options for closing the Bulge, the least ambitious of which was a push by VII Corps to coincide with Patton's offensive, meeting forces near Houfallize. While it would cut off any German forces in the deepest pockets of the Bulge to the northwest of Bastogne, most senior commanders realized it would trap few German forces. Eisenhower approved the plan on 27 December with Patton's Third Army to jump off on 30 December and First Army to start counterattacks on 3 January. This approach meant pushing the Germans out of the Bulge, rather than trapping them within and counted on attrition rather than envelopment to destroy Wehrmacht units.

After several days of inconclusive skirmishing around the Bastogne perimeter, and considerable repositioning of forces, both sides planned major attacks on 30 December. Middleton's VIII Corps had been reinforced and consisted of the 87th Division to the west, the newly arrived and green 11th Armored Division in the center and the 9th Armored Division at the base of the corridor. The aim of this attack was to begin to push the German forces away from the western side of Bastogne. At the same time, Manteuffel planned a three-phase assault, beginning with an attack by the 47th Panzer Corps against the corridor from the northwest and the new 39th Panzer Corps from the southeast.

Both sides exchanged heavy artillery fire in anticipation of the attacks, and both the 11th Armored Division and 87th Division made modest gains. Remer's Fuhrer Begliet Brigade hardly got past its start point and the neighboring 3rd Panzergrenadier Division was tied down in defensive operations for most of the day. The attack by the 39th Panzer Corps with a Kampfgruppe of the 1st SS-Panzer Division and the newly arrived 167th VG Div. struck the US 35th Division around Lutrebois. The US infantry defended tenaciously, and were backed by divisional artillery, the artillery of the 4th Armored Division and significant close air support. General Höcker of the 167th VG Div. reported that his lead battalion was "cut to pieces … by tree smasher shells", the new and secret US Army proximity fuses debuted at Bastogne that detonated at predetermined altitudes over the ground, substantially improving their lethality against exposed infantry. When the main Panzer column of the 1st SS-Panzer

Division Kampfgruppe moved into action around noon, it was pummeled by air attack along the Lutremange-Lutrebois road. A Panzer company that escaped the *Jabos* stumbled into an ambush of the 4th Armored Division and was stopped after losing about a dozen tanks and three assault guns. By the end of the day, the German attacks had completely failed and the momentum was clearly shifting to the American side.

A planned 6th Armored Division attack on 31 December from the eastern side of the corridor, became trapped by icy roads and the congested road network. The attack began in earnest on New Year's Day, making good progress with the capture of Bizory and Mageret, and progress was even better on 2 January. The division's neighbor, the 35th Division, was slow in joining the attack due to the need to clear out remaining pockets of German resistance from the attack the preceding day. The VIII Corps continued to push up along the right side of Bastogne, with the tanks of the 11th Armored Division slugging it out in a series of skirmishes with Remer's Führer Begleit Brigade. In four days of fighting, the 11th Armored Division advanced only six miles at a cost of 660 casualties, 42 M4 and 12 M5A1 tanks. Nevertheless, the VII Corps had stopped the 49th Panzer Corps attack cold, and its capture of the road junction at Mande-St Etienne threatened to cut off the German forces on the northwest side of Bastogne.

With his own prospects for offensive action now gone, Manteuffel was so worried that the American advances on the west side of Bastogne might trap the 47th Panzer Corps that he recommended a general pull-back to the line Odeigne–La Roche–St Hubert. While Model agreed, he knew that Hitler would countenance no retreat. In later years, Manteuffel pointed to the 3 January 1945 fighting as the final turning point in the Ardennes

An M4 medium tank of the 4th Armored Division takes part in operations to push out of Bastogne on 3 January 1945 with a .30cal. machine-gun team in the foreground. (NARA)

A view inside Bastogne on 20 January as a truck column of the 90th Division passes through. (NARA)

when the strategic initiative passed entirely to the US side. After this date, the Wehrmacht was never again able to stage a significant attack in the Ardennes and for the most part endured a series of grinding defensive battles.

ERASING THE BULGE

By late December, even Hitler had given up hope of victory in the Ardennes. On 27 December, the 6th Panzer Army was ordered to go over to the defensive. Hitler's enthusiasms turned in another direction, to Alsace, hoping to exploit the overextended defensive lines of the US 6th Army Group there, which had been stretched to cover part of the line formerly held by Patton's Third Army. Operation Nordwind was launched on 3 January 1945, gaining some initial successes. But it had no strategic consequences, and little impact in the Ardennes beyond placing even more stringent limits on German reinforcements and supplies. Manteuffel asked Model on 2 January to authorize a general withdrawal from the Bastogne vicinity to a more defensible line hinged on Houfallize, but Model knew of Hitler's opposition to any withdrawal and so refused. Hitler instead ordered another attack on Bastogne for 4 January, which fizzled after only minor gains. The US First Army began its offensive operations to join up with Patton's Third Army on 3 January 1945. On 5 January, Model was forced to pull out two of the Panzer divisions from the Bastogne sector to reinforce the badly pressed 6th Panzer Army, ending any further attempts against Bastogne.

From the American perspective, the early January fighting was as much against the weather as against the Germans. The snowy conditions grew progressively worse, and the struggles for the many small road junctions between Bastogne and Houfallize were bitter and costly for both sides. On 8 January, Hitler recognized the obvious, and authorized a withdrawal to prevent German units from being trapped by the slow but steady American advance. But the withdrawal did not proceed as planned, and La Roche was captured sooner than anticipated. Hitler planned to gradually have the 5th Panzer Army take over the 6th Panzer Army sector, with the 6th Panzer Army serving as a reserve to counter an anticipated Allied attack at the base of the Bulge, the type of operation proposed by Patton that was not in fact in the works. However, other events intervened. The fighting in the Ardennes became irrelevant on 12 January 1945 when the Red Army launched its long-expected winter offensive. With the Red Army on Germany's doorstep, there were no longer any resources for Hitler's foolish gambles in the west.

On 14 January, Rundstedt himself pleaded with Hitler to permit a withdrawal in stages all the way to the Rhine, but Hitler would only countenance a withdrawal to the Westwall. On 16 January, the US Third and First Armies met at Houfallize, marking the end of the first phase of erasing the Bulge. It would take until 28 January to recapture all of the territory lost to the German offensive.

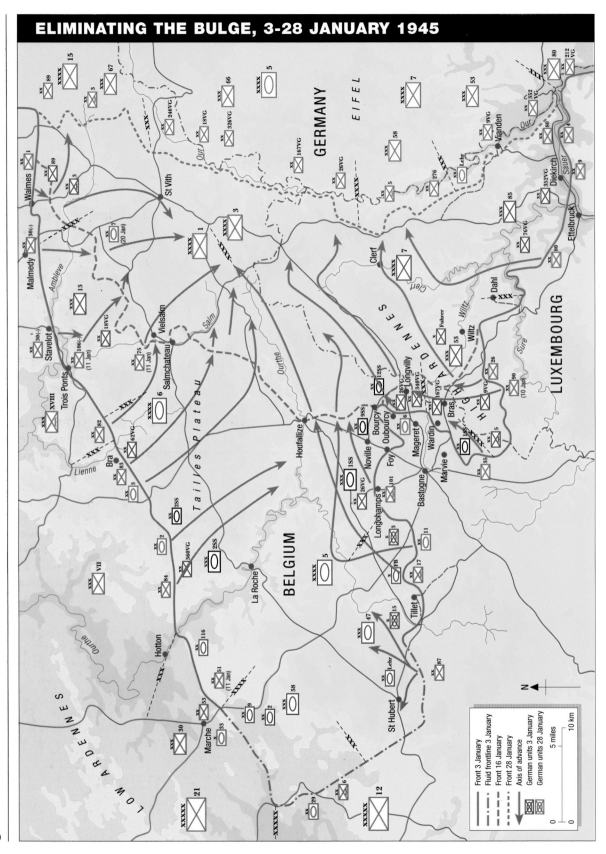

90

THE AFTERMATH

Hitler's final gamble in the West had failed within its first week when the 6th Panzer Army was unable to secure the Meuse River bridges at Liege. Although the 5th Panzer Army had far greater success in penetrating the American defenses in the central and southern sector, this was a race to nowhere that was operationally irrelevant as it neither destroyed any significant US forces nor did it secure any vital terrain. At best, the Ardennes attack disrupted the pace of Allied offensives into western Germany, but even this is debatable since the attrition of the Wehrmacht in the Ardennes weakened later defensive efforts in 1945. The most significant strategic effect of the Ardennes offensive was to distract German attention from the growing threat of Soviet offensive actions. The drain of resources to the west prevented the creation of viable reserves to counter the predictable Red Army assault into central Germany in mid-January 1945, helping to ensure the disaster that followed.

From a tactical perspective, the performance of Manteuffel's 5th Panzer Army clearly outshone Dietrich's 6th Panzer Army. When the US Army in 1995 used historical data from the Ardennes offensive to test one of their computer war game simulations, the war game concluded that the 5th Panzer Army had performed better than expected, and the 6th Panzer Army more poorly than its resources would have suggested. The Waffen-SS continued to suffer from mediocre leadership at senior levels, which was particularly evident in offensive operations such as the Ardennes. In contrast, the regular army continued to display a high level of tactical excellence even under the trying circumstances of the Ardennes operation, epitomized by Manteuffel's superior leadership in preparing and executing the badly flawed Ardennes plan. Nevertheless, the emaciated Wehrmacht of late 1944 did not have the combat

For months after the battle, the Belgian countryside was littered with wrecked armored vehicles. This is a knocked-out German Sd.Kfz. 251/9 (7.5cm) "Stummel" used to provide fire support for Panzergrenadier units, and photographed by the US Army Howell mission. (NARA)

effectiveness in offensive operations of years past. The head of Rundstedt's staff later wrote that the Ardennes had "broken the backbone of the Wehrmacht on the western front". A meeting at Model's headquarters after the fighting concluded that morale had plummeted since the defeat, and "the German soldier is in general fed up." The head of the Luftwaffe fighter force, Adolf Galland later wrote that the Luftwaffe was "decimated in the large air battles, especially during Christmas and finally destroyed" during the Ardennes campaign. As the diarist of the Wehrmacht High Command, P.E. Schramm later noted, "The abortive (Ardennes) offensive had made it clear not only the aerial but the armored superiority of the enemy."

Losses in the Ardennes fighting were heavy on both sides. US casualties totaled 75,482 of which there were 8,407 killed, 46,170 wounded and 20,905 missing through the end of January. The British XXX Corps lost 1,408 including 200 killed, 239 wounded and 969 missing. Estimates of German losses vary from about 67,200 to 98,025 casualties depending on the parameters. In the case of the lower of the figures, this included 11,171 killed, 34,439 wounded and 23,150 missing. The Wehrmacht lost about 610 tanks and assault guns in the Ardennes, or about 45 percent of their original strength, compared to about 730 US tanks and tank destroyers.

Although the US Army suffered from some serious mistakes by senior commanders at the outset of the offensive, at the tactical level, its units performed well. The only division to be completely overwhelmed, the 106th Division near St Vith, was a green unit in an exposed and badly overextended position, overwhelmed by more numerous enemy forces. The American response to the German offensive was timely and effective, exploiting the US advantage in battlefield mobility to quickly shift units to block the German advance. The stalwart defense by US infantry, armor and engineer units, backed by ample artillery support, stopped the German offensive.

From an operational perspective, the Allied response after Christmas was lackluster with the exception of Patton's prompt relief of Bastogne. Bradley and Eisenhower suffered a blow to their confidence by failing to anticipate the German offensive. Combined with the unfortunate decision to allow Montgomery to control the US forces in the northern sector of the front, the Allied counterattack was timid and failed to exploit the potential either to trap significant German forces or at least to force a less organized withdrawal. In spite of these problems, the US Army's defeat of the Wehrmacht in the Ardennes crippled the Wehrmacht in the West and facilitated the offensive operations into northwestern Germany in February and March 1945.

The Ardennes campaign precipitated a crisis in Allied command after Montgomery made a number of tactless remarks that exaggerated his own role in the victory. Montgomery had been campaigning for months to be named the supreme land forces commander as part of a broader effort to shift Allied strategic planning towards his view that the offensive against Germany should be conducted on a narrow front by his own 21st Army Group. Eisenhower considered asking for his resignation as the best solution to this nagging problem and Montgomery backed down, largely ending the Allied debate about the strategic conduct of the war in northwest Europe in Eisenhower's favor.

THE BATTLEFIELD TODAY

The Battle of the Bulge devastated the small towns in the Ardennes, and much has been rebuilt since the war. Rural communities such as these do not change quickly, and while the roads are much better than in 1944, the terrain features are much the same. Some of the wooded areas have changed little, and there is still evidence of the trenches and dugouts from the fighting. A set of good road maps is an absolute must, as it is easy to get lost in the maze of small roads. Having been made famous by the battle, Bastogne commemorates the fighting with many memorials and several museums. The city is ringed with US Sherman turrets destroyed during the fighting, and placed on stone pedestals to mark the outer boundaries of the defenses in 1944. In McAuliffe Square in the center of town sits an M4 tank, *Barracuda* of the 41st Tank Battalion, 11th Armored Division, knocked out on 30 December 1944 near Rechimont, and recovered after the war. The Bastogne Historical Center outside town is one of the best of the many Battle of the Bulge museums and has an exceptional collection of uniforms and equipment. There are many tanks and other items of equipment scattered around this section of Belgium, in mute testimony to the battle. A trip to neighboring Luxembourg is also highly recommended, although its present-day scenic beauty belies the difficulties faced by the soldiers fighting there in the winter of 1944–45. The National Military History Museum in Diekirch is devoted to the Battle of the Bulge, and has an excellent collection of vehicles, equipment, and uniforms.

This Panther Ausf. G tank, probably from the 116th Panzer Division, was recovered after the fighting and is preserved in a park near the main street of Houfallize. (Author's collection)

BIBLIOGRAPHY

Due to its importance, the Battle of the Bulge has been the subject of hundreds of books, especially from the American perspective. The defense of Bastogne has been the focus of a disproportionate share of the books, not only because of the drama of the story, but due to the tendency to pay special attention to the units remaining under Bradley's control and less to those units under Montgomery.

This book was heavily based on unpublished material as well. The best perspective on the German side is provided by the scores of interviews conducted with nearly all the senior German commanders by the US Army after the war as part of the Foreign Military Studies effort. Copies of these are available at several locations including the US Army Military History Institute at Carlisle Barracks, Pennsylvania, and the US National Archives in College Park, Maryland. Some of these have been reprinted in two books edited by Danny Parker: *Hitler's Ardennes Offensive* and *The Battle of the Bulge: The German View* (Greenhill and Stackpole, 1997, 1999). Besides the many wartime, after-action reports, there are a large number of unpublished US Army studies of the battle including *Armor under Adverse Conditions: 2nd and 3rd Armored Divisions in the Ardennes* (Ft. Knox, 1949) and *Armor at Bastogne* (Ft. Knox, 1949). There are numerous divisional histories of the units fighting in the Ardennes, and Battery Press has reprinted many of the best of these including the superb 101st Airborne history *Rendezvous with Destiny* and other useful accounts such as the 28th Division history.

Statistical data on the battle comes from a number of sources including *Ardennes Campaign Statistics: 16 December 1944–19 January 1945* prepared by Royce Thompson (OCMH, 1952). In addition, in the early 1990s, the US Army Concept Analysis Agency commissioned the creation of a very large statistical database on the campaign to test its computerized Stochastic Concepts Evaluation Model, a computer war simulation program. This database was based on extensive archival research and provides day-by-day data on personnel, casualties, and weapons strength on both sides.

Cavanagh, William, *A Tour of the Bulge Battlefield*, (Leo Cooper, 2001). A good, short history of the Ardennes campaign along with useful information on making a battlefield tour by one of the acknowledged experts on the battle.

Cole, Hugh M., *The Ardennes: Battle of the Bulge*, (OCMH: 1965). This US Army official history in the Green Book series still remains the best single volume on the battle, and is still in print through the US GPO.

Gaul, Roland, *The Battle of the Bulge in Luxembourg*, (Schiffer, 1995). A highly detailed two volume account of combat operations in Luxembourg with Volume 1 covering the Germans and Volume 2 the Americans.

Guderian, Heinz Gunther, *From Normandy to the Ruhr*, (Aberjona, 2001). A candid and highly detailed account of the 116th Panzer Division by a veteran of the unit and son of the famous German Panzer commander.

Jung, Hermann, *Die Ardennen-Offensive 1944/45*. (Musterschmidt, 1971). The classic German account of the Ardennes campaign.

Koch, Oscar, *G-2: Intelligence for Patton*, (Schiffer, 1999). The memoirs of Patton's intelligence chief which reveals the controversy about the Allied intelligence blunders at the beginning of the Battle of the Bulge.

Koskimaki, George, *The Battered Bastards of Bastogne*, (Casemate, 2003). A collection of interviews with veterans of the 101st Airborne about the defense of Bastogne by the radio operator of the divisional commander.

Marshall, S.L.A., *Bastogne: The First Eight Days*, (Infantry Journal 1946, 1988 GPO reprint). A detailed account by the army historian, based on battlefield interviews with the American participants.

Pallud, Jean Paul, *Battle of the Bulge: Then and Now*, (After the Battle, 1984). The definitive photographic history of the battle by the well-known specialist, that combines extensive historical photos with contemporary photos of the same scenes. A smaller companion volume by Philip Vorwald was published in 2000.

Parker, Danny, *To Win the Winter Sky*, (Combined Publishing, 1994). An excellent account of the air war over the Ardennes.

Reynolds, Michael, *Sons of the Reich: II SS Panzer Corps*, (Casemate, 2002). An account of the II SS-Panzer Corps in 1944–45 with extensive coverage of the Ardennes campaign.

Ritgen, Helmut, *The Western Front 1944: Memoirs of a Panzer Lehr Officer*, (Federowicz, 1995). A first hand account of Panzer operations by a colonel of the Panzer Lehr Division, including operations in the Ardennes.

Winter, George, *Manhay: The Ardennes, Christmas 1944*, (Federowicz, 1990). A short but informative monograph on the fighting between the 7th Armored Division and the 2nd SS-Panzer Division based on interviews with veterans from both sides.

INDEX